Praise for the work of Roland

"Another unusual police procedural is Rolando Hinojosa's realistic-feeling *Ask a Policeman*. As this case about cross-border murder and drug-smuggling unravels, Hinojosa gets to you in his sneaky way. He's witty about the Orwellian bylaws in the middle-class neighborhoods of Klail City, Texas . . . and once in a while he nails a character with a single line of dialogue. Hinojosa is also mordantly funny about the local law enforcement honchos who queue up at the U.S. federal trough."

—*The Washington Post* on *Ask a Policeman*

"Rolando Hinojosa has established himself as sole owner and proprietor of fictional Belken County, which, like the author's native Mercedes, is situated in the Lower Rio Grande Valley. If Belken is the Lone Star Yoknapatawpha, Hinojosa is its Faulkner."

—*The Texas Observer* on *Ask a Policeman: A Rafe Buenrostro Mystery*

"The timeless truths of war—the slaughter of civilians, atrocities condoned, legions of refugees—are related with near-documentary realism in this powerful novel of the Korean War. Hinojosa draws on his own experience in Korea to reveal the racism that Mexican Americans faced from fellow soldiers. Hinojosa gives us a graphic picture of the unchanging face of war—raw, gritty and inhumane."

—*Publishers Weekly* on *The Useless Servants*

"Hinojosa's novel is in the form of a diary kept by a young Mexican-American soldier serving in the Korean War. Its spare style, heavily spiced with military lingo, and episodic form are intended to recreate the fragmented process of discovery that occurs when one is at war. But what the narrator, Rafe Buenrostro, discovers is not heroism or patriotism, but the futility of war and its heavy human toll."

—*Booklist* on *The Useless Servants*

"Like Faulkner, [Hinojosa] has created a fictional county (Belken County), invested it with centuries of complex history, and populated it with generations of families and a host of unique characters. The saga is a rich mosaic, and Hinojosa renders the collective social history of a Chicano community. Hinojosa's tack in this novel is to dramatize how the community responds to *la mujer nueva*, the Chicana who eschews traditional roles and asserts her independence and individuality. [He] spins the story of Becky and her twenty-five friends and enemies with sensitivity, humor, wit and keen insight into the history and attitudes of the people of the lower Rio Grande Valley of Texas."

—*World Literature Today* on *Becky and Her Friends*

"Hinojosa turns his Faulknerian gaze upon a particular family struggle, in this case a divorce. It is an opportunity to observe a master of voice and characterization at work, to watch a web-spinner weave a narrative masterpiece."

—The Texas Observer on *Becky and Her Friends*

"Themes which predominate and are explored in a humorous, good natured fashion include: the migration experience of Texan Mexicans, family feuds, the ongoing conflict between Anglos and Mexicans and the experiences of Mexicans in the Korean conflict and the Second World War. While Hinojosa explores the exploitation of Texas Mexicans at the hands of Anglos, his message is never heavy-handed or didactic, but rather pointed and understated. Hinojosa has an unusual talent for capturing the language and spirit of his subject matter."

—Western American Literature on *Klail City*

"Hinojosa's *Dear Rafe* effectively uncovers social, economic and political relationships along the Texas border. A mystery of sorts, it permits readers to make their own judgments about the reality of Klail City. The dozens of characters speaking in their own voices create not a babble but a sort of call and response pattern between cultures, classes and generations. With a quiet irony and persistent understatement, Hinojosa describes an alien place that is part of who we are as a people."

—Newsday on *Dear Rafe*

"Hinojosa's obvious and heartfelt feminism, his linguistic facility, erudite allusions and, above all, his witty, colloquial, epigrammatic pronouncements make this novel a feast for scholars." *—Choice* on *Dear Rafe*

"*Rites and Witnesses* has delighted and mystified [Hinojosa's] audience. In the very ambiguity of the documents, his purpose becomes known. The issues are clear, the battle lines are drawn, the reader now knows that what is at stake is the death of a culture." *—Houston Chronicle* on *Rites and Witnesses*

"*Partners in Crime* reads like Dashiell Hammett with a Texas twang, but underneath it all is Hinojosa's gift for conversational lyricism. . . . a brilliant technical achievement." *—Dallas Morning News* on *Partners in Crime*

A Voice
of My
Own
Essays and Stories

Rolando Hinojosa

WITH AN INTRODUCTION BY
HÉCTOR CALDERÓN

Arte Público Press
Houston, Texas

A Voice of My Own: Essays and Stories is made possible through a grant from the City of Houston through the Houston Arts Alliance.

Recovering the past, creating the future

Arte Público Press
University of Houston
452 Cullen Performance Hall
Houston, Texas 77204-2004

Cover design by Pilar Espino
Rolando Hinojosa-Smith outside the Harry Ransom Center at The University of Texas at Austin. Photo by Marsha Miller.

Hinojosa, Rolando
  A Voice of My Own : Essays and Stories / by Rolando Hinojosa ; with an introduction by Héctor Calderón.
    p. cm.
  ISBN 978-1-55885-712-4 (alk. paper)
    I. Calderón, Héctor. II. Title.
  PS3558.I545V65 2012
  814'.54—dc23
                                                      2011037907
                                                           CIP

∞ The paper used in this publication meets the requirements of the American National Standard for Information Sciences—Permanence of Paper for Printed Library Materials, ANSI Z39.48-1984.

11 12 13 14 15 16 17 18   10 9 8 7 6 5 4 3 2 1

CONTENTS

— Introduction—

vii | The Many Lives of Rolando Hinojosa

— Essays—

1   A Voice of One's Own

9   This Writer's Sense of Place

17   Living on the River

35   E Pluribus Vitae

39   Breve pesquisa del Valle del Río Grande

45   Puentes

49   De noche todos los inmigrantes son pardos, con excepciones

55   Ni con gasolina

59   Crossing the Line: The Construction of a Poem

73   '50s Austin: A Variform Education

81   The Gulf Oil-Can Santa Claus

87   A Few Notes on Translation

93   Chicano Literature: An American Literature with a Difference

99   Redefining American Literature

105 The Baroque in the Life and Literature of the Hispano-American

— Stories—

117 Es el agua (Spanish)

123 *Es el agua* (English)

129 El puñal de Borges

133 Nice Climate, Miami

INTRODUCTION:
THE MANY LIVES OF ROLANDO HINOJOSA

I recall first meeting Rolando Hinojosa in the early 1980s at an MLA (Modern Language Association) National Convention. He had just delivered a paper at a panel and was answering questions in the hallway just as he was leaving. Besides beginning a career as a writer, Hinojosa was one of the first Chicano professor activists advocating for the inclusion of Chicano literature within the MLA. I was waiting in line to introduce myself. I had just begun my career as an assistant professor. A Chicano graduate student had questioned, in a more critical than inquisitive tone, why Hinojosa just wrote about one county in Texas. That Hinojosa had, obviously, read widely in many literatures did not matter to the student. Or that other writers like James Joyce, William Faulkner, Juan Rulfo and Gabriel García Márquez had chosen to write about their own fictional corner of the world did not matter either. Hinojosa smiled back without any anger and responded that he was happy with his county and did not see a need to change that. Hinojosa had two published novels in the United States at that time, *Estampas del valle y otras obras* (1973) and *Generaciones y semblanzas* (1977). We did not yet know his expanding literary corner of the world, Belken County, Texas. As is well known, Hinojosa has continued with his *Klail City Death Trip Series* through some eleven install-ments; his latest *We Happy Few* was published in 2006.

Hinojosa is a Chicano writer who spans the entire tradition, one of the founding members of what is termed the Quinto Sol Generation. He received the third annual Premio Quinto Sol for Novel in 1973. This is now ancient history of which many of my current graduate and all of my undergraduate students are not aware. In his *We Happy Few,* Hinojosa enters the world of campus politics, faculty promotions and tenure at Belken State University. In his first two novels of the 1970s, readers were introduced in Spanish to nineteenth-century Texas Mexicano ranching culture and the deaths of elder Mexicanos who passed away in mid-twentieth century. This then is a developing history that Hinojosa has been writing in a variety of literary forms, chronicle, bio-graphical sketch, epistolary novel, diary, detective fiction, comedy and poetry all told through monologues, conversations, dialogues with his characteristic wit, humor and irony. Needless to say, Hino-josa is one of the tradition's canonical writers.

But it should be clear that becoming canonical was not an easy matter for the first generation of Chicano writers or those who were Chicanos or Mexicanos before the Chicano Movement. Becoming a student, an academic, a professor and a writer had its strange turns and twists. The many lives of Rolando Hinojosa began before the Chicano Movement as a teenager in the moun-tains above Saltillo, Coahuila, in a Mexican rural environment where he wrote his first stories, which were in Spanish; upon returning from Mexico, Hinojosa joined the army and served in Korea; the citizen soldier returned to Texas for undergraduate study at the University of Texas, Austin in the 1950s; he earned an M.A. at New Mexico Highlands University in 1963 and a Ph.D. at the University of Illinois in 1969, both advanced degrees were in

Spanish literature. He was a "Chicano scholar" before the Chicano Movement.

A Voice of My Own: Essays and Stories is a parallel volume to Hinojosa's fragmented history of Belken County. Those who know Hinojosa's fiction understand his own use of time. Readers, more often than not, are left in medias res, looking at the past from an indeterminate present and anticipating a future yet to be told. This constancy of change can occur within as well as between books. In *A Voice of My Own*, Hinojosa's life is more fully fleshed out, certainly as a writer, but also as son, student, high school teacher, civil servant, office manager, sales manager, laborer, professor, university administrator, translator and as a Texas Mexicano from the Rio Grande Valley who has lived through decades of change. There is much useful personal and institutional history in this volume that can take the reader back to the *Klail City Death Trip Series*.

A Voice of My Own presents a collection of essays spanning some three decades. History, place, language and the border are the constant interrelated themes of the essays. Hinojosa is a product of the first northern Mexican settlers in the Spanish Province of Nuevo Santander established in 1749 which along the Rio Grande would become the cradle of ranching culture in the United States. This history has nurtured a sense of place based not on cattle and horsemen but on relationships among family and friends, a way of looking at the world from a disadvantaged position given the history of Texas but with a certainty of self and cultural identity. Like Hinojosa in these essays, his characters survey the situation, the problem and arrive at decisions, conclusions in a rational manner. Loud, blustery voices are not part of his characters nor of Hinojosa's voice.

The early settlers brought with them northern Mexican Spanish which has remained constant through the twenty-first century. I am pleased that *A Voice of My Own* includes essays in Spanish. In 2011, Spanish is a personal as well a public language, of oral expression as well as literary expression in the United States. Hinojosa makes it clear in this volume that literature in Spanish had existed in Texas before the Chicano Movement of the 1960s. As then, this language continues to unify Spanish-speakers across the jurisdictional barrier between Mexico and the United States. Hinojosa says it often in this collection; the border was never a cultural barrier. In the initial essay, "A Voice of One's Own," Hinojosa responded to Richard Rodriguez's *Hunter of Memory* (1981), to his shame of being Mexican, the son of Spanish-speaking parents, so much so that Rodriguez advocated against bilingual education and the use of Spanish as a public language. With Rodriguez in mind, Hinojosa wrote "I wonder about those who choose adaptation over true happiness in a desire to please others; and I wonder, but not for very long, about those who ignore, and about those who choose to deny the existence of at least two cultures" (4-5). Hinojosa's parents, Manuel G. Hinojosa and Carrie Effie Smith, like other Mexican and Anglo families and marriages from the Valley, both spoke Spanish and English. Hinojosa is the finest exponent in literature of the duality and fusion of these two cultures.

The border as a political barrier between two cultures has existed since 1835—the Texas Republic. The subsequent War of 1848, Hinojosa writes, created the Valley, el Valle which is Texas (in the past Union and Confederate) north of the Rio Grande but always will be Mexican which also means that social and racial strife will continue to condition relations among cultures be they Mexican, Anglo or African American. In addition to wars on Mexican-U.S. soil and in Korea, Hinojosa recalls the Mexican Revolution of 1910. After the celebrations of the centennial of the Revolution, it will serve us well to emphasize that this Mexican civil war declared in San Antonio was a northern Mexican phenomenon that also included Texas Mexicanos. As we discover in this volume in "E Pluribus Vitae," Don Manuel G. Hinojosa, like other Mexicanos del Valle, supported the Mexican Revolution. Throughout Hinojosa's fiction, the Revolution has been a constant—his first short story written in the 1940s as a youth in Coahuila was based on events in the Revolution. As in 1910 with Mexican émigrés in el Valle recalled by Hinojosa, Mexican immigrants have continued in waves after waves to enter the United States and el Valle. Let's now in 2011 state clearly that Hinojosa is an American writer, a Texas writer, a Chicano writer and a writer of the Mexican cultural diaspora of North America.

Rolando Hinojosa and I did eventually meet at that MLA Convention. I was patient and took my turn. Readers of *A Voice of My Own* will find a voice that has remained constant in his fiction, in these essays and in his lives. Rolando is a friend and through the years the profession has brought us together in Germesheim, Paris, Aix-en-Provence, New Haven, Austin, Palo Alto, Claremont and Los Angeles. I have relied on his knowledge as an administrator, scholar, writer and friend. He has always been generous with his time, support and advice. Most recently, he expressed his condolences for my recent personal losses. I thank him here publicly. In the very insightful "The Baroque in the Life and Literature of the Hispano-American," Hinojosa speaks of the brevity of life as the most Baroque of all elements. Life is "[i]n brief, a one-way trip where we all share the same destination if not the same estimated time of departure" (111). The solemnity of death, the passing away of time and life, is acknowledged in his Baroque novel, the *Klail City Death Trip Series*, in the essays collected here in this volume and, personally, in our friendship. These essays in *A Voice of My Own* whether in the form of personal recollection, biographical sketch, short story or literary criticism are all delivered with that unmistakable Hinojosa style—direct, personal, witty and honest. The voice does not vary. It's the one I heard in that hallway many years ago.

ESSAYS

A VOICE OF ONE'S OWN
(1982)

Texas Library Association (TLA) San Antonio, TX

I make no claim to a privileged position in regard to living in two cultures or within two cultures or, even, *between* two cultures. I happen to think and to observe that most of us who reside in Texas live in various cultures, anyway. And, if one is to believe the latest U.S. Census Report in regard to the population makeup of Texas, there are some 2.9 million Texas Mexicans who are residents of this state. Of that number, then, I'd hazard the claim that some ninety-five percent—an arbitrary figure—are bound by both cultures. But, by the same token, and in varying degrees of intensity in acculturation and assimilation, many Anglo Texans and Black Texans are also living in a bicultural environment.

It's a busy two-way street this thoroughfare of ours, and, as is well known, no one group can live and work in proximity to another without developing some cultural as well as some psychological bonds. Now, that some people do not recognize this, or that they choose to ignore this, or that they choose to deny this fact, nevertheless, the fact remains. Eustace Budgell, a minor figure in English history, once remarked that facts are bothersome things in that they refuse to go away. Bonds exist.

The following is a fact of unperceived biculturalism: In this city, the Ignacio Lozano family, through its newspaper, *La Prensa*, and through its other publications as well as through its own publishing house, maintained a Texas Hispanic tradition in arts and letters for over fifty years. And not only here in San Antonio, but also throughout the state. That the majority population, that is, the solely English-speaking population, did not recognize this does not and did not alter the fact that *La Prensa* and thus Texas Mexican letters existed and enjoyed rude health.

That distribution was carried on a daily basis for those fifty years, that Mexican national writers as well as homegrown Texas Mexicans contributed to its literary pages (as my present colleague, Américo Paredes, did, as a young poet some forty years ago) may have been ignored by the rest of Texas, but this too, did not and does not alter the fact of *La Prensa*'s long and lively existence.

The inheritors of this half-century of literary tradition were well served by this tradition in Texas, and when their sons and daughters began to write and to publish in Spanish, or in English, or in both languages as a matter of conscious choice, and then began calling it Chicano Literature, it didn't matter if there were denials of its existence—the facts, proof and evidence of its existence were and are both palpable and available. And because of subsequent creativity, publication and distribution, those who buy and read the texts enjoy the two cultures which are, after all, inextricably bound. As professional librarians, I'm sure that you noticed the omission of the words *acquisition* and *cataloguing* when I mentioned creativity, publication and distribution.

Let me assure you that I and other writers can take care of the first; that friends and colleagues such as Professors Kanellos and Rodríguez* can handle the publication and the distribution of it,

---

*Publisher Nicolás Kanellos and distributor Juan Rodríguez were panelists with Hinojosa at this Texas Library Association session.

but it is you—and no one else—who is responsible for acquisition, cataloguing and, eventually, the assigning of shelf space for this literature. And this is your charge since one can neither ignore nor deny the existence of this American literature. All of us live within two cultures—in varying degrees, as I said, and whatever the degree, the two cultures are inescapable.

I speak neither in rancor nor in disappointment; a learned society such as yours needs no preaching of truths since librarians and no one else in or out of the academy are the maintainers and the keepers of the keys to the libraries, those repositories of learning without which no nation can either survive or call itself free. Yours, then, is a most serious responsibility.

When I was first asked to consider speaking before you in the Summer of 1982, I asked, among other things, what the topic would be. The topic would be the two cultures. I also took it upon myself that this also meant the lack of awareness and the omissions in Texas' cultures, and I'll tell you why: One of the courses I teach at the University is *Life and Literature of the Southwest*. The number for the course is E 342, an upper-division course populated, mostly, by graduating seniors. We read George Sessions Perry, Américo Paredes, Fred Gipson, Katherine Anne Porter, Tomás Rivera and Larry McMurtry, among others. Prior to my coming to the University on a full-time basis, no Texas Mexican writers were read in that course; it was a simple omission and nothing personal since Texas Mexican writers were already included in similar courses in as disparate universities as Texas A&M, North Texas State University, Tarleton State University and the like. A simple omission, as I said, and one that was corrected without fanfare.

The chief reason presented for the inclusion of the Texas Mexican writers—and their talent demanded it—lay in the question, how, then, can one conduct classes about Texas literature, in a course devised years ago by J. Frank Dobie, which do not include the writings of and about those Texans who comprise an important part of Texas history and culture? A similar question could be raised for our public and school libraries and their hold-ings if such omissions exist.

On a personal note, the very fact of my being the issue of my Texas Mexican father and his Anglo Texas wife, and because of my long life in Texas, I have seen and lived in both cultures from a first-hand experience. But it has also been my experience to note a certain reticence by some to recognize the worth of the seemingly parallel cultures in Texas life. As a few of you may know, I was born in the Valley; I was nurtured there and educated there both in Mexican and in American Schools. One language supplanted the other for a while, but eventually they balanced each other out. What developed from this, among other matters, was an idiosyncratic vision of the world; an awareness of differences and similarities. What I worked on, as far as my life was concerned, was toward a personal voice which was to become my public voice.

What you see here, this professor, and what ideas I may pre-sent, is what you will see in my writings: the voice doesn't vary —I was not ashamed of my parents after I received my education, for I was not ashamed of them before I acquired one; I never ran out of things to say to them because of my education nor did they to me because of theirs. And neither of them spoke in hushed, soft-Spanish voices as some Chicano writers describe those who speak that often strident and vowel-filled language. In short, they were my parents, and I their son, and I was not going to write about them or about our mutual cultures as if they were pieces of some half-baked mosaic. A mosaic envisioned, and worse, fos-tered, by some publishing houses which should know better, and do, but who rather choose not to when it comes to selling their books as products and not as conveyors of ideas or truths in respect to this population group.

I come from those cultures, I'm a product—albeit not a fin-ished one, yet—of them, I cannot be anything else, and I choose not to be anything else other than what I am.

At times, I wonder about those who choose adaptation over true happiness in a desire to please others; and I wonder, but not for very long, about those who ignore, and about those who choose to deny the existence of at least two cultures and of the complex symbiotic relationship inherent in the various Texas cultures. It must be a strange world, this ostrich-like existence and attitude which flies—bottoms up, if I may—against evidentiary proof.

When I was invited to speak on two cultures I was also somewhat befuddled, as no less a figure than Virginia Woolf was befuddled when she was asked to talk on women in literature. In both our cases, there was so much to say and so little time to say it in. Added to this, in her case, she didn't know if she were to be anecdotal about Jane Austen, the Bröntes, Fanny Burney and Miss Mitford or if she were to talk about women characters in English literature. She decided that what women needed, and lacked, was a room of one's own. And she wrote on that. Recalling that fine introduction of hers to her little book of the same title, I wondered what the host had in mind. Was I to be anecdotal? Entertaining? Educational? Or what? As you must know, or suspect, putting oneself in the position of wanting to please the audience is the first step toward abdicating one's position and ideas. I decided that wouldn't do; if I were to accept the invitation, make the time to sit and write an acceptable paper, from my point of view, then I would have to devote the necessary time to think about the vast, the humorous and the often sad contradictions in Texas; but to embark on that ship and journey lies madness since twenty minutes is hardly the realistic time to list, let alone to comment upon, our shared history and culture. Whatever I did decide, though, it was to be with one's own voice.

What also helped in my decision to accept and to write this paper was that this was not my first talk to librarians on an allied subject: Mexican-American literature, which is part and parcel of our Texas culture. Remembering that meeting, I decided to accept the invitation. That talk was given years ago when Mexican-American literature was struggling for inclusion in higher education; that time is now past, and now many of us spend time tightening up, shoring up and continually working up newer themes and topics and dropping others, as one does in the continuous revision of higher education curricula, until the subject is hammered into workable shape. (In a parenthetical remark, I've mentioned the word *decision* no less than half a dozen times here, but you see, it so happens that writing is a decision, and not to be taken lightly).

As to my qualifications to speak on two cultures and on literature of the Southwest, time will take care of that piece of business. Time is the ultimate judge, not I, and not you. Time is also the great leveller, and all of us in this room, myself included, will succumb to time and not all of us in this room will see the end of this century, a mere seventeen-years away. On that somber but realistic note, I'll end my long-winded introduction and begin my brief remarks which deal with my experience as a writer and to personalize my literary career, to quote from the letter of instruction sent by the TLA.

I have been writing rather seriously since the age of fifteen, and I had my first acceptance—three of them, in fact—in high school in Mercedes, Texas. It concerned an annual literary event called *Creative Bits*. These writings were bound and, as far as I know, they were still available some ten years ago, for those curious enough to see them, in the Mercedes High School library.

My first paid publication, on the other hand, appears twenty-seven years later in V. 3, Spring 1972 of the journal *El Grito*. Since then, I've published six books and some sixty-plus briefer works of prose, poetry and assorted critical essays on literature. My publishing career, then, has been brief but feverish.

In my case, it seems that a prolonged drought has been followed by a torrent. I by no means advocate this as a guide for those who wish to write, or, worse still, for those who wish to see their names in print. It just happens to be my case, and since I am unable to alter my life, I accept the way it is turning out. So much, then, for publications.

What do I write about? I write about what I assume other writers write about: that which they know. I happen to know something about people and about how some of us are. I happen to know some history about the Valley, this country, the state. And I happen to work toward improving and maintaining a grip on memory and events. Add to this two lifetimes, one of observation and participation, and another of unsystematic but enjoyable reading, and you'll see that idiosyncratic vision I mentioned earlier, and you'll be able to read the personal and public voices as well as the voices of those hundreds of characters who populate the works: the fair and the mean, the fools and knaves, the heroes and cowards, those who are selfish, and those who are full of self-abnegation in a place called Belken County, of which I'm the sole owner and proprietor, as Faulkner once said when he spoke of his county.

My published career, then, is going on its eleventh year. Because of this, my experiences as a writer are not worth accounting for. It is the time of my childhood and young manhood that have served me well in my writing; that, and a somewhat sketchy education, an interestingly remarkable home life, and with neither apologies nor bombast, the ability to sit down and write, to rewrite and to keep at it, until I am both satisfied and convinced that nothing more can be added or deleted to whatever it is I'm writing.

These concluding remarks have been mercifully brief for you and me. Thinking back on my life, I found that talking about writing produced very little of it; I decided at one point to cut down on talking and to concentrate on writing. I think it was a wise choice for me.

I am, primarily, a professor of literature, but my writing has increased my capacity for life, and I hope that this has helped my students.

To sum up, I also consider myself a reader and a lover of books; my first school job was that of librarian in the fourth grade in North Ward Elementary in Mercedes; I know the name's been changed, but it will always be North Ward to me. My college job was a four-year stint in the Reserve Reading Room at the University of Texas; I gravitated to those jobs, as you may have already guessed by now, by the example set at home by parents who read to themselves and to each other and who—not once—ever ordered us to read something or—if in the act of reading—not once denigrated the book or the choice of our reading material. I keep reminding myself of this whenever I see my children read whatever it is they read.

In conclusion, I am now convinced that I am a reader who decides to write until the opportunity to read again becomes available.

THIS WRITER'S SENSE OF PLACE

(1983)

I begin with a quote from a man imprisoned for his participation in the Texas-Santa Fe Expedition of 1841; while in his cell in Mexico City, he spurned Santa Anna's offer of freedom in exchange for renouncing the Republic of Texas. Those words of 1842 were said by a man who had signed the Texas Declaration of Independence and who had served in the Congress of the Republic. Later on, he was to cast a delegate vote for annexation and contributed to the writing of the first state constitution. He would win election to the state legislature and still later he would support secession.

And this is what he said:

> I have sworn to be a good Texan; and that I will not forswear. I will die for that which I firmly believe, for I know it is just and right. One life is a small price for a cause so great. As I fought, so shall I be willing to die. I will never forsake Texas and her cause. I am her son.

The words were written by José Antonio Navarro. A Texas historian named James Wilson once wrote that Navarro's name is virtually unknown to Texas school children and, for the most part, unknown to their teachers as well. A lifetime of living in my native land leads me to believe that Professor Wilson is correct in his assessment of the lack of knowledge of this place in which we were born and in which some of us still live.

The year 1985 marks the one hundredth anniversary of the birth of my father, Manuel Guzmán Hinojosa, in the Campacuás Ranch, some three miles north of Mercedes, down in the Valley; his father was born on that ranch as was his father's father. On the maternal side, my mother arrived in the Valley at the age of six weeks in the year 1887 along with one of the first Anglo-American settlers enticed to the mid-Valley by Jim Wells, one of the early developers on the northern bank. As you may already know, it's no accident that Jim Wells County in South Texas is named for him.

One of the earliest stories I heard about Grandfather Smith was a supposed conversation he held with Lawyer Wells. You are being asked to imagine the month of July in the Valley with no air conditioning in 1887; Wells was extolling the Valley and he said that all it needed was a little water and a few good people. My grandfather replied, "Well, that's all Hell needs, too." The story is apocryphal; it has to be. But living in the Valley, and hearing that type of story laid the foundation for what I later learned was to give me a sense of place. By that I do not mean that I had a feel for the place; no, not at all. I had a sense of it, and by that I mean that I was not learning about the culture of the Valley, but living it, forming part of it, and thus, contributing to it.

But a place is merely that until it is populated, and once populated, the histories of the place and its people begin. For me and mine, history began in 1749 when the first colonists began moving into the southern and northern banks of the Rio Grande. That river was not yet a jurisdictional barrier and was not to be until almost one hundred years later; but, by then, the border had its own history, its own culture and its own sense of place: it was Nuevo Santander, named for old Santander in the Spanish Peninsula.

The last names were similar up and down on both banks of the river, and as second and third cousins were allowed to marry, this further promulgated and propagated blood relationships and that sense of belonging that led the Borderers to label their fellow Mexicans who came from the interior, as *fuereños,* or outsiders; and later, when the people from the North started coming to the Border, these were labeled *gringos,* a word for foreigner, and nothing else, until the *gringo* himself, from all evidence, took the term as a pejorative label.

For me, then, part of a sense of the Border came from sharing: the sharing of names, of places, of a common history and of belonging to the place; one attended funerals, was taken to cemeteries, and one saw names that corresponded to one's own or to one's friends and neighbors, and relatives.

When I first started to write, and being what we call "empapado," which translates as drenched, imbibed, soaked or drunk with the place, I had to eschew the romanticism and the sentimentalism that tend to blind the unwary, that get in the way of truth. It's no great revelation when I say that romanticism and sentimentalism tend to corrupt clear thinking as well. The Border wasn't paradise, and it didn't have to be; but it was more than paradise, it was home (and as Frost once wrote, home, when you have to go there, is the place where they have to take you in).

And the Border was home; and it was also the home of the petty officeholder elected by an uninformed citizenry; a home for bossism and for old-time smuggling as a way of life for some. But, it also maintained the remains of a social democracy that cried out for independence, for a desire to be left alone and for the continuance of a sense of community.

The history one learned there was an oral one and somewhat akin to the oral religion brought by the original colonials. Many of my generation were raised with the music written and composed by Valley people, and we learned the ballads of the Border little knowing that it was a true native art form. And one was also raised and steeped in the stories and exploits of Juan Nepomuceno Cortina, in the nineteenth century, and with stories of the Texas Rangers in that century and of other Ranger stories in this century and then, as always, names, familiar patronymics: Jacinto Treviño, Aniceto Pizaña, the Seditionists of 1915 who had camped in Mercedes, and where my father would take me and show and mark for me the spot where the Seditionists had camped and barbecued their meat half a generation before. These were men of flesh and bone who lived and died there in Mercedes, in the Valley. And then there were the stories of the Revolution of 1910, and of the participation in it for the next ten years off and on by Valley *mexicanos* who fought alongside their south bank relatives, and the stories told to me and to those of my generation by exiles, men and women from Mexico, who earned a living by teaching us school on the northern bank while they bided their time to return to Mexico.

But we didn't return to Mexico; we didn't have to; we were Borderers with a living and unifying culture born of conflict with another culture and this, too, helped to cement further still the knowing exactly where one came from and from whom one was descended.

The language, too, was a unifier and as strong an element as there is in fixing one's sense of place; the language of the Border is a derivative of the Spanish language of Northern Mexico, a language wherein some nouns and other grammatical complements were no longer used in the Spanish Peninsula, but which persisted there; and the more the linguistically uninformed went out of their way to denigrate the language, the stiffer the resistance to maintain it and to nurture it on the northern bank. And the uninformed failed, of course, for theirs was a momentary diversion while one was committed to its preservation; the price that many Texas Mexicans paid for keeping the language and the sense of place has been exorbitant.

As Borderers, the north bank Border Mexican couldn't, to repeat a popular phrase, "go back to where you came from." The

Borderer was there and had been before the interlopers; but what of the indigenous population prior to the 1749 settlement? Since Nuevo Santander was never under the presidio system and since its citizens did not build missions that trapped and stultified the indigenous people, they remained there and, in time, settled down or were absorbed by the colonial population and thus the phrase hurled at the Border Mexican "go back to where you came from" was, to use another popular term, "inoperative." And this, too, fostered that sense of place.

For the writer—this writer—a sense of place was not a matter of importance; it became essential. And so much so that my stories are not held together by the *peripeteia* or the plot as much as *by what* the people who populate the stories say and how they say it, how they look at the world out and the world in; and the works, then, become studies of perceptions and values and decisions reached by them because of those perceptions and values which in turn were fashioned and forged by the place and its history.

What I am saying here is not to be taken to mean that it is impossible for a writer to write about a place, its history and its people, if the writer is not from that particular place; it can be done, and it has been done. What I *am* saying is that I needed a sense of place, and that this helped me no end in the way that, I would say, Américo Paredes in *With His Pistol in His Hand,* Larry McMurtry in *Horseman, Pass By,* Fred Gipson in *Hound Dog Man,* William Owens in that fine, strong *This Stubborn Soil* and Tomás Rivera in . . . *and the earth did not part* were all helped by a sense of place. And I say this, because to me, these writers and others impart a sense of place and a sense of truth about the place and about the values of that place. Theirs isn't a studied attitude, but rather one of a certain love, to use that phrase, and an understanding for the place that they captured in print for themselves; something that was, for themselves, then, at that time and there. A sense of place, as Newark, New Jersey, is for Phillip Roth, and thus we see him surprised at himself when he tells us he dates a *schicksa,* and then, the wonderful storyteller that he is, he tells us of his

Jewish traditions and conflicts, and we note that it becomes a pattern in some of his writings whenever he writes of relationships, which, after all, is what writers usually write about: relationships. I am not making a medieval pitch for the shoemaker to stick to his last here, but if the writer places a lifetime of living in a work, the writer sometimes finds it difficult to remove the place of provenance from the writings, irrespective of where he situates his stories. That's a strong statement and one which may elicit comment or disagreement, but what spine one has is formed early in life, and it is formed at a specific place; later on when one grows up, one may mythicize, adopt a persona, become an actor, restructure family history, but the original facts of one's formation remain as facts always do.

It's clear, then, that I am not speaking of the formula novel, nor is it my intent to denigrate it or its practitioners; far from it. I consider the formula novel as a fine art, if done well, and many of us know that they do exist. I speak of something else—neither nobler nor better, no—merely different from that genre. It's a personal thing, because I found that after many years of hesitancy, and fits and spurts, and false starts, that despite what education I had acquired, I was still limited in many ways; that whatever I attempted to write, came out false and frail. Now, I know I wanted to write, had to write, was burning to write and all of those things that some writers say to some garden clubs, but the truth and heart of the matter was that I did not know where to begin; and there it was again, that adverb of place, the *where;* and then I got lucky: I decided to write whatever it was I had, in Spanish, and I decided to set it on the border, in the Valley.

As reduced as that space was, it too was Texas with all of its contradictions and its often repeated one-sided telling of Texas history. When the characters stayed in the Spanish-speaking milieu or society, the Spanish language worked well, and then it was in the natural order of things that English made its entrance when the characters strayed or found themselves in Anglo institutions; in cases where both cultures would come into contact, both languages were used, and I would employ both, and where one and only one would do, I would follow that as well. What dominated, then, was the place, at first. Later on I discovered that generational and class differences also dictated not only usage but which language as well. From this came the *how* they said *what* they said. As the census rolls filled up in the works, so did some distinguishing features, characteristics, viewpoints, values, decisions, and thus I used the Valley and the Border, and the history and the people. The freedom to do this also led me to use the folklore and the anthropology of the Valley and to use whatever literary form I desired and saw fit to use to tell my stories: dialogs, duologs, monologs, imaginary newspaper clippings and whatever else I felt would be of use. And it *was* the Valley, but it remained forever Texas. At the same time, I could see this Valley, this border, and I drew a map, and this, too, was another key, and this led to more work and to more characters in that place.

It was a matter of luck in some ways, as I said, but mostly it was the proper historical moment; it came along, and I took what had been there for some time, but which I had not been able to see, since I had not fully developed a sense of place; I had left the Valley for the service, for formal university training and for a series of very odd jobs, only to return to it in my writing.

I have mentioned values and decisions; as I see them, these are matters inculcated by one's elders first, by one's acquaintances later on and usually under the influence of one's society which is another way of saying one's place of origin. Genetic structure may enter into holding on to certain values and perhaps in the manner of reaching decisions, for all I know. Ortega y Gasset, among others, I suspect, wrote that man makes dozens of decisions every day, and that the process helps man to make and to reach more serious, deliberate and even important decisions when the time presents itself. A preparatory stage, as it were. The point of this is that my decision to write what I write and where I choose to situate the writing is not based on anything else other than to write about what I know, the place I know, the language used, the values held. When someone mentions universality, I say that what happens to my characters happens to other peoples of the world at given times, and I've no doubt on that score. What has helped me to write has also been a certain amount of questionable self-education, a long and fairly misspent youth in the eyes of some, an acceptance of certain facts and some misrepresentations of the past which I could not change, but which led to a rejection not of those unalterable facts but of hypocrisy and the smugness of the self-satisfied. For this and other personal reasons, humor creeps into my writing once in a while, because it was the use of irony, as many of us know, that allowed the Borderer to survive and to maintain a certain measure of dignity.

Serious writing is deliberate as well as a consequence of an arrived-to decision; what one does with it may be of value or not, but I believe that one's fidelity to history is the first step to fixing a sense of place, whether that place is a worldwide arena or a corner of it, as is mine.

LIVING ON THE RIVER
(1995)

I n Texas, as it has for a million years or so, the Rio Grande runs
down from somewhere in El Paso to its mouth, just south and
east of Brownsville, where it dies peacefully enough in Boca
Chica as it empties into the Gulf of Mexico; geologists call it an
old river and to prove it, they will point to the countless meanders
of the Rio Grande as it wends its way to the Gulf. Meanders also
produce the drowned portions of the river which are called *resacas*
in the Valley; the word is now an English-language borrowing and
known to native Texas Mexicans and Anglos alike. Language borrowings, of course, are part of the daily life of any area where two
countries come together, and I will touch on this later on. For now,
mention must be made on the general Texas Anglo attitude regarding Spanish and Spanish usage by Texas Mexicans in the Valley.

Texas Anglos have long denigrated the language as not being
Castilian; what they don't know is that the language *is* Castilian; it
differs in pronunciation and borrowings from that of Spain as the
Spanish spoken in Argentina also differs from that of Spain. What

the majority of them don't know as well is that Spain has many other languages within the Peninsula (Aragonese, Valencian, Galician and those spoken with greater frequency in the Basque country and Catalonia). The truth of it all is that they don't care to think matters out; to many of them, if the Texas Mexicans speak Spanish, then it must be of an inferior kind, a sort of bastard Spanish, as it were. This is a matter of cultural superiority on the part of too many Texas Anglos and is based not on linguistic knowledge but on ignorance and its corollaries: racial bias, prejudice and discrimination.*

Any border presents different faces to non-borderers, and borders also tend to be self-sufficient in some regards; in the Valley, the ordinary citizenry on both banks of the Rio Grande looks askance, in some ways, to the federal capitals of Mexico and the United States. A result is that they focus on their immediate area. Too, the countries present different laws; in the United States federal laws are set by precedent, while in Mexico, the Napoleonic code and its modifications prevail. And so, as most border communities, the topographic barriers are jurisdictional but not necessarily cultural. Added to which, because of the relative isolation of the area (from, say, roughly 1747 to 1848) there was a forging of a new culture, not necessarily one hundred percent Mexican nor one hundred percent American. As is the usual case in most cultures, those aspects of the culture which have proved cumbersome or displeasing have been modified by the borderers. These changes, obviously, cut across the river and across societal lines.

Language, a part of culture, also changed in time, but it's been the Texas Mexican who has remained firm for the most part to Spanish while, at the same time, adopting English and then modifying both languages as time goes on.

Fear must be added to this list: fear of miscegenation (as if they were of purer blood), and fear of discovery of their own shortcomings of whatever stripe. This last fear, as being less than perfect in the eyes of Mexican Americans, must have presented a heavy burden, although the local weekly newspaper took care not to mention scandals among the Mercedes Texas Anglo society. Still, Mercedes was a small town and secrets are among the last things that people keep in such places.

This is not to claim that that part of Texas and Mexico has forged a new language; but it is to say, that the original Spanish language brought to the area by the first settlers in 1747 has been maintained and modified, and then enlarged through time by the additions during the nineteenth and twentieth centuries through the printed word and later by radio and television.

The region's Spanish language, then, has kept the fundamental base and syntax while, at the same time, reflecting those changes which are a part and parcel of any living language. Had the original Valley Spanish remained unchanged from the mid-seventeenth century version, then we would have with us the vestiges of a dead language, that is, one that did not admit borrowings from other languages which is, primarily, the cause of a language to wither. As an instance, in contemporary times, Romansch, spoken still in parts of Switzerland, is a European example of a Stagnant and about-to-disappear language.

Marriages, and I will not go into marriage customs, often take place by those who cross from one side of the river to the other, and thus relations are sustained legally and by blood. It is not for me to say how strong or how warm and close the kinships are since this depends on each individual family. I am well aware, of course, of the Mexican-American myth which claims family warmth and how Roman Catholicism influence couples not to divorce. To believe either one of those myths is illusory now as it was in years past.

Divorce among this predominantly Roman Catholic population is not uncommon anymore.

Marriage unions, however, bring us to the interesting points of names. My hometown, Mercedes, Texas (Hidalgo County), in the 1940s, had a population of 6400, and the Hinojosa-Smiths were but one family whose parents carried Spanish and non-Spanish names.

I will not pretend I knew each family of Mexican and Anglo parentage, but the following are ones I do remember living in Mercedes: Baum, Billings, Bowman, Brooks, Carr, Carroll, Closner, Foley, Gavlin, Handy, Heath, Howell, January, Johnson, McGee,

McVey, Moody, Parker, Postell, Pue, Rowland, Starcke, Thomas and Werbiski. There may have been others.

There are several points here, however. The numbers have increased since my time, and I would put this down to the historical inevitabilities of any borderland. Too, intermarriage is not an in-frequent phenomenon in most border areas. However, I do not wish to leave the impression that these families either shared similar interests with each other or looked at themselves as different or as special because of the special parentage. For me, attending the same elementary, junior high and high school with these family members bore this out. The majority, it should be obvious, carried the paternal last names first, while we and others carried the Spanish name first in the Hispanic manner.

The following surnames represent but a few of similar marriages up and down the Valley: Atkinson, Chamberlain, Hatcher, Hon, Hull, Kingsbury, Putegnat, Ramsey, Randolph, Rutledge, Solitaire, Trdla and Turner. Across the river, a cursory look at the Matamoros and Reynosa, Tamaulipas, telephone directory immediately reveals such names as Brawn, Brockman, Kelly, Schu and so on.

Was there racial discrimination on the Texas side? the answer is yes, and it is also a complicated *yes* for one noticed, indeed, one couldn't help but notice, that some Texas Anglos also discriminated socially against other Texas Anglos. The same applied (and applies) among Texas Mexicans, particularly those in the professional class who looked (and look) down upon other Texas Mexicans.

Texas Anglos and Texas Mexicans also forged business and law partnerships, and while this was not uncommon, it was also not the norm.

That was then. As matters stand now, the Texas Anglos are a distinct numerical population minority in the Rio Grande Valley.

The student school population ranges anywhere from 70 percent to 95 percent Texas Mexican; the administrators and the schoolroom teachers stand at sixty to seventy percent Texas Mexican in the over seventy cities and towns that dot that part of the state from Brownsville (Cameron County) to Rio Grande City

(Starr County). Similar figures go for the athletic coaches and directors of the independent school districts in the area.

Needless to say, the school boards of education range from 100 hundred percent to 75 percent Texas Mexican members. When it comes to municipal governments, there are some four Texas Anglo mayors at present; the city councils are also over-whelmingly Texas Mexican. The same goes for other elected officials such as county commissioners, county judges, district attorneys and so on.

In brief, the infrastructure, businesses and the free professions (e.g., doctors, dentists, attorneys, accountants) are also in the majority. This is something that began to develop after World War II and Korea and the sixties with the many-sided civil rights movements.

When it comes to financial institutions, banks and savings and loan companies, these were the last to fall, as it were, but they have come into line as far as board of directorships, ownerships, partnerships and other bank officials.

Whether one was Texas Anglo or Texas Mexican, no one who was raised during the Depression could envision the current state of affairs. It is not (and is it ever?) peaches and cream in the Rio Grande Valley for it is usually listed as one of the poorest areas in the United States, as it should be since it's a simple truth. It is as poor, say, as are Vermont, Maine and New Hampshire, where unemployment, in this year of 1995, stands at twenty percent.

Those states are also border states, although one should not infer that they are poor as a consequence of being border states.

Now, I know it is an article of faith when one writes about Texas Mexicans in the Rio Grande Valley that one must point out racial injustice, discrimination and prejudice. I think it is just that one do so, but I also think it incumbent on one to repeat that Texas Mexicans also discriminate against their own. For if skin color is often an important determinant in the United States, the color of one's skin is also a matter of importance in the Valley.

The naked truth is that we come in all colors, personalities, characters, weaknesses, strong points and so on.

In the Valley border area, our general attitude toward Afro-Americans can be briefly stated by mentioning but two epithets directed against them: *mayate* (black beetle) and *tinto* (inky), as well as anti-Afro-American Spanish-language racial jokes and English-language jokes borrowed from the Texas Anglos. While these may not be strong enough as evidence for some, the shameful (there is no other word) late nineteenth- and early twentieth-century behavior by border Mexican nationals and by Texas Mexicans against Afro-American soldiers stationed in Brownsville should be.

After months of suffering personal indignities against themselves and their wives, the black soldiers protested and defended themselves physically in Matamoros, Tamaulipas, Mexico, and in Brownsville. The newspaper called it a riot (instigated, the papers said, "by colored troops"), and those not jailed, were hunted down. The upshot was that over two dozen of them were dishonorably discharged; President Theodore Roosevelt refused them a plea of clemency, and the sentences stood for over fifty years.

El Puente de los Negros is what Texas Mexicans call the bridge (*Nigger Bridge* is what Texas Anglos call it) where the black soldiers took refuge when elements of the U.S. Army, along with civilians and county city officers gunned some of them down. This took place in Brownsville, Texas, the same Brownsville where a one-room schoolhouse served as the black school for some years after the *Brown v. Board of Education* decision of 1954.

This is not to say that all Texas Mexicans are racist, but it is to say that we should recognize our faults in racial matters. The same goes for Texas Anglos; not all are racists, obviously, but in my youth, in Mercedes (and in the other Valley towns without exception) racism was a given. So much so that during the Depression, despite money being scarce in the Valley, the Mission, Texas board of education built a second high school exclusively for Texas Mexicans. This in a jackleg town of less than 12,000 inhabitants.

Changes have occurred since, of course, and the former Chairman of the House Committee on Agriculture is a resident of Mission: the Honorable Eligio (Kika) de la Garza, Democrat from Texas. In passing, to show another part of the changes, the other three congressmen for the area from southern San Antonio down to Laredo and then down the river to the Valley and up the coast to Corpus Christi are all Spanish-surnamed: Gonzalez, Ortiz and Bonilla.

Congressman de la Garza may be typical, in many ways, of the old Valley families: he was born in Mercedes, raised in Mission and married Lucille Alamía of Edinburg, all three in Hidalgo County.

In my youth, Texas was a one-party state: solid Democrat. Or as is said in some circles, Yellow-dog Democrats. The term comes from an apocryphal story that a Texan was such a Democrat that he would rather vote for a yellow dog than for a Republican. This, too, has changed since the Republicans now rule the state in Austin and Washington, D.C.

The point, though, is that Texas was solid Democrat and goes to prove how much of a southern state it was despite one of the state's strongest myths that it was a western, hence, cowboy state. Hollywood made it a cowboy state, of course, for prior to the Civil War, Texas was a slave-holding state and accordingly seceded from the Union. After the war, it underwent Reconstruction, it also instituted the poll tax to prevent blacks from voting, and it provided separate tax-based facilities to separate the races in schools, hospitals and in public transportation. And, as in any Southern state, private transport also provided for separate seating and toilet facilities for non-Anglos. This was not merely a Southern custom, this was a state-legislated mandate.

Part of the Valley was, as some other parts of Texas, in sympathy with the Union during the Civil War. Further up river, Laredo, a part of South Texas but not the Valley, was decidedly on the Confederate side with Captain Santos Benavides taking part in that war as did his opponent, the guerrilla leader, the Valleyite Octaviano Zapata, who fought for the Union. Mexican nationals from the border also volunteered and served in the Union army.

In the Valley, many Texas Anglos who sympathized with the South during the Civil War tried the same discriminatory tactics with Texas Mexicans and met with some success. Southern racial discriminatory practices and influences lasted even during World War II, and cities such as Harlingen and McAllen, to name but two, did not allow Texas Mexicans in the municipal public swimming pools or schools while at the same time, other towns did not discriminate. Since many of the towns were divided either by the railroad tracks (Mercedes, Weslaco, Donna and others) into Texas Anglo town and Mexican town, other elected officials relied on zoning laws and division of precincts with a predominantly or exclusively Texas Anglo or Texas Mexican population.

Again, one has to point out that this was not a universal in the Valley. While I attended North Ward Elementary School, a 100 percent Texas Mexican school with Anglo teachers, South Ward was predominantly Texas Anglo, but not wholly, since many Texas Mexican families lived on the south side of the railroad tracks and thus were enrolled in South Ward. The early separation came to naught, however, since Mercedes had but one middle school (grades seven to eight) and one high school (grades nine through twelve), which were attended by both groups.

As for the three black youngsters of school age in Mercedes, they were bussed to McAllen, twenty miles away for high school or to Harlingen, fourteen miles away, to the elementary grades.

The Catholic elementary school admitted both Texas Mexicans and Texas Anglos, but there was discrimination there as well: one of the Texas German Catholic families saw to it that Anglo and Mexican school children were to be taught in separate rooms. This took place in the twenties, and my parents reacted immediately by disenrolling my oldest sister, Clarissa; unfortunately, they were the only parents to do so. Clarissa was then enrolled in North Ward Elementary, where the lone Texas Mexican teacher was Miss Mary Ann Villarreal, who taught in the second grade.

There may have been discrimination on the part of our Anglo teachers in middle and high school, and while one was always sensitive to being left out of school functions, we were nevertheless included. There was, though, separation: in the school dances, and each group stayed apart.

Dating was something else. In my time, during the forties, some Anglo girls dated Mexican boys, although I never knew of Anglo boys who dated Mexican girls. Still, at a recent school reunion, I saw some old Anglo schoolmates who married Mexican women. So, in keeping with border living, the practice of this type of marriages between the two groups continues now as it had in the past.

Post-high school education in the Valley started with two junior colleges in 1927: one for the lower Valley, Brownsville, and one for the upper Valley in Edinburg, each with an Anglo higher administration and faculty.

In 1951, Pan American College was established in Edinburg and is now called The University of Texas-Pan American. With its current president, a native Texas Mexican, there has been a substantial increase in the number of Texas Mexicans in both administration and faculty.

Not long after World War II, Brownsville Junior College became Texas Southmost College but remained a two-year school. The institution is now called The University of Texas at Brownsville; it must be pointed out that neither institution calls for the same admission standards as The University of Texas at Austin.

Because of this and residual racism, Texas Anglos in the Valley refer to both institutions as Taco Tech, Tamale College, Spick University, among other unhappy names, and those who can afford it, prefer to send their university-eligible sons and daughters elsewhere.

Despite the pejorative name-calling, repeated personal visits reveal high morale among students and faculty. Most of the student body is first-generation college, and are typical Valleyites: quite secure as to who they are, thus they have little doubt as to their identity. One reason I adhere to the Mercedes experience is not that it was unique in any way; it was my experience but not too different from the majority of Valley border towns during that time.

Even if we didn't experience discrimination at first hand or on a daily basis, racial prejudice was there, and we reminded ourselves that it was there.*

What we had, both societies, that is, were separate structures. Not necessarily parallel however. For instance, Mercedes published the *Enterprise* once a week and it was read, predominantly, by the Anglo residents. It was a typical small-town newspaper with notes about book clubs, garden societies, visits from out-of-town relatives and such typical fare. Unless the War Department sent a telegram to the family (and to the Mercedes *Enterprise* for propaganda purposes in order to unify the citizenry as Americans), few to no Texas Mexican names appeared in the paper. Those that did, did so usually at semester's end when some of us made the scholastic Honor Roll or when some of us graduated from high school. During the school year, Spanish surnames would also appear when some of us participated in athletic events, school plays or any other extra curricular activity. In the main, however, the *Enterprise* was their newspaper, not ours.†

And now? The tilt is inescapable; due to the 90 percent Texas Mexican population; the ads for restaurants, garages, car dealerships and other business establishments are for and by Texas Mexicans. It's a Texas Mexican town; the older Texas Anglo generation still publishes its announcements regarding the book clubs, the garden societies and so on, and this will go on until they die out. As for their sons and daughters and grandsons and granddaughters, the majority no longer live there. The same, however, is also true for many Texas Mexicans who moved away and whose presence has been replaced by Mexican nationals who, in time, have become American citizens.

---

*Gender prejudice has to be included since this mental construct appears in most societies, including that of the Mexican American. That Mexican-American males may ignore the fact; it must be pointed out that they were not the usual objects of rape, incest or of other forms of espousal and parental abuse.

†In Mercedes, as in other Valley towns (among them Brownsville, Weslaco and Mission), some Mexican Americans owned their own small presses. Through them, part of the culture was preserved by way of *corridos*, broadsides and the occasional satirical publication, *calaveras*.

Change, as always, is the only constant.

The change in the political landscape has been mentioned, and I will touch on that again: it used to be that when Texas was a one-party state, the Democratic as said, there would be one effective election for the candidates, the primary election. Whoever won that one, won the general election since it was always Democrats against Democrats with no Republican opponents available.

It worked this way: 30-inch by 40-inch yellow-colored sample ballots would be printed by the county government. Each ballot would contain the office and the list of people running for office, and these would be posted all over town by the precinct chairmen. Election judges would then be appointed, and when election time came for the primaries (after the barbecues, the speeches, the usual promises, etc.), the voting would take place. Whoever won the primaries, as just mentioned, was the sure winner for the general elections to be held five months hence. In case of a run-off election, usually the highest two, at times, the highest three candidates, would hold an election and the winner would then take office after the general elections.

A sweet arrangement for the ins, obviously. Texas Mexican names one would see would be for the office of constable; this was usually an assured payment for helping the successful sheriff during the campaign.

After World War II, in Mercedes, Rodolfo Garza and Jesús Salinas ran for city commissioner posts. When Texas Mexicans first started running for public office in the thirties, it was usually countered in this manner: say there were two Texas Mexicans running for one office; in that case, one Texas Anglo would run against them and defeat both, since the Texas Mexican vote would be divided and the Texas Anglos would vote for their candidate.

In the case of Garza and Salinas, however, they ran as a team: that is, each one ran for a different city commissioner's post. They won. As is usual in politics, they began to form alliances with the Anglo officeholders on various issues. In time, that is the way that Mercedes politics were changed. When its population increased, and the voting populace became predominantly Texas Mexican. A result is that Texas Mexicans run against each other, as in the old days, but with a difference: the overwhelming Texas Mexican population can still out-vote the Texas Anglo candidate.

That is the way it is now and has been for the last thirty years. Will it continue? The chances are very good that it will: the border is still porous, newer immigrants, legal or not, continue to cross the river, many professional Mexicans live on the American side, their children attend American schools and become Americanized. This last is gospel: the boys and girls, Mexican citizens still and thus pay tuition to enroll in school, participate in school functions, become cheerleaders, play football and so on. They are in the process of acculturation and assimilation; their parents may not speak much English, in the way of the older American citizens of Mexican descent who didn't either, but they too, if not assimilated, are acculturating daily.

This is an interesting phenomenon and one not much taken into consideration by many recent Mexican-American scholars unfamiliar with the area, its culture and most of its history.

Has the overwhelming election of Rio Grande Valley Texas Mexican public officials brought Texas Mexicans a step nearer to the kingdom of heaven on earth?

Hardly. Venality is not necessarily a universal Texas Anglo trait nor is honesty a Texas Mexican monopoly.*

---

*In the 1980s, the Texas Anglo district attorney for a Valley county was removed for malfeasance; and, it is not uncommon for former county attorneys, after they leave office, to represent drug smugglers. In the recent case of Brígido Marmolejo, former sheriff for Hidalgo County, he was convicted on charges of bribery, and other crimes, and is now serving time in federal prison. At present, mid-summer of 1995, a Texas Mexican county judge is also under criminal indictment. And just four years ago, a Texas Mexican former member of the U.S. Congress was also convicted of federal crimes.

And no, it isn't a matter of the Anglos going after Texas Mexican officials, given that the vast majority of state and federal judges, and members of the juries, are Texas Mexicans. Perhaps a quote from Saul Alinsky would help. During a successful attempt at organizing the unorganized, he was asked how they would fare once in power. His reply was: "Oh, they'll all probably turn out to be shits."

Nowadays, school boards with a 100 percent Texas Mexican membership may (and do) hire and fire Texas Mexican superintendents, principals and teachers, usually without regard to name, race, blood or culture. They may do it on a whim or on personal enmity or regard, or whatever it pleases the board to call its collective mind. One thing the hired and fired can't do is complain that the action was taken because of racial prejudice.

Such, too, is the case in other spheres, business, for one.

In the forties, when it was such a triumph in the Valley for a Texas Mexican to work for an Anglo enterprise such as a public utility or, as a clerk or secretary for a law firm, it was considered an advancement. It was more likely an economic advancement as well, but it was a legitimate breakthrough, and it was so, and due, in great part, to being, in the early days, a high school graduate, and later, a college graduate.

Whatever educational weaknesses existed then, and exist now, that road has been one well-traveled by Valley Texas Mexicans. Education did not bring happiness nor was it intended to do, I don't think. But the older generations knew that education was what they did not have and something, then, that their children would have to have in order to compete. (Tomás Rivera in his . . . *y no se lo tragó la tierra* at times alludes, at other times points, to education as one means of advancement; education with all its travails and disappointments, to be sure, was something, *anything*, that was an improvement and better than the life being led at the time).

For many Valley Texas Mexicans of my generation (I was born in 1929), our first schooling (and this includes Rivera, a native, not of the Valley but of the Winter Garden area) was in the form of private schools owned and operated by Mexican men and women, exiled in Texas during one phase or another of the Mexican Revolution. These were our first schools and meant to be followed later by the public schools, or, in some cases, by parochial schools. Current events were read of in *La Prensa*, the Spanish-language daily published San Antonio and delivered by rail all over Texas.

The above, of course, helped to maintain a Hispanic presence in the state; for the Valley, with relatives living just across the river, with our easy access to Argentine, Cuban, Mexican and Spanish films on the Texas side, and the schools just mentioned, emphasized one's Mexicanness; true, much of the myth came along with it, but Spanish-language newspapers and radio also helped to steep one in Mexican history.

Added to all of this is the long history of Texas Mexicans in the region (since the 1749 settlement by Escandón on both sides of the river after his exploration and surveying of the area during 1747-48). Furthermore, the area was and remained decidedly rural for a century and a half; this, along with the preceding, afforded one the opportunity to know the area, its history and our relationship with Mexico and the United States. That the following generations know little of Mexican history is not to be deplored; it's the way of the world and the way of subsequent generations to rely on myths and not on facts. In brief, family histories are pleasant enough, but they mustn't muscle out the historical truths and tragedies faced by Texas Mexicans after 1848.

The majority of our fellow Texans also rely on myths, and this, of course, goes for the newer Anglo Texans, those who have moved there to evade harsh winters and, at times, to relocate due to employment opportunities. That they learn to distrust Mexicans or to consider us as lesser beings or as less than reliable is understandable given that their initial friendships are formed by Texans steeled in myths about us, about the state and about their own worth. It's laughable to Valley folk when the newer Texans talk about roots, but such an attitude by Texas Mexicans also betrays a certain smugness on our part.

In the end, when everyone dies, nothing is important, really. Marriages, intermarriages, wars, economic deprivation, missed opportunities for understanding or reconciliation, hatred, racial prejudice and all other matters which at times unite and at times disunite us, will mean nothing when one dies.

If the Valley has given me anything, and it's given me much, it has given me a clear picture of what it is to die; the Army just focused it some, but it was the Valley with its old cemeteries on both sides of the river which has formed, cemented for the most part, my view of life.

The careful reader will have noticed I said "cemeteries on both sides of the river" and not "cemeteries on both sides of the border." The border is a term usually employed by non-borderers. And, when we speak in Spanish we always mention "el río" but not "la frontera." *La frontera*, or the frontier, is used by those who live in inland territory. We, borderers, usually say "across" or "this side" or "the other side" (with *the river* or *of the river* being the implied phrase).

The border is a defining place, a separateness of citizenship, even, but it may, to outsiders, also imply a separate culture. It shouldn't, and it doesn't do so in the Rio Grande Valley.

It isn't that we are special; most of the preceding certainly attests we aren't. What we are, though, is a culture group that was isolated for a century and a half on land that was contested by many sides for a long time until after Reconstruction, and then forced to assimilate and acculturate while, at the same time, being relegated to a nonassimilative and nonaccalurative status. That last is obviously a contradiction, but such is life, if it's to have any meaning.

After all, a life without contradictions is not a life worth living and enjoying. Some years back, when the majority of voters in California voted English as the official language, the Texas governor, Republican William Clements, made life interesting once again. As soon as the Californians voted to make English their official language, Governor Clements said no such law would be passed in Texas while he was governor. The heroic Texas legislature kept quiet, which is also a contradiction.

That many suffered and will continue to suffer indignities on both sides of the river is a given. But there had to be some happiness along the way in the midst of suffering: love, children, friendships, self-sacrifice, standing up to be counted and all those things that make life worth living despite our neighbors who live on both sides of the river.

It must be emphasized that many Mexican nationals also discriminated again Mexican Americans: excoriated our language, our way of life, our culture and, in their eyes, our lack of one is a matter of public record.

But it is also a matter of public record that various Mexican governments protested against the ill-treatment of American citizens of Mexican descent who suffered and underwent discrimination and, at times, lynchings, at the hands of their fellow American citizens.

We were not alone, then, not altogether, were we?

That Octavio Paz wrote that wrong-headed article on the Zootsuiters and whatever else the splendid novelist wrote about Mexican Americans in general was in part right; he couldn't help it. But that he was wrong much more of the time is certainly the case. One of the things wrong about our attitude toward Paz is that we should recognize that he was enjoying the first amendment rights under this country's Constitution, the right to be wrong at the top of one's voice.

What is also wrong is to attack him at this late date; that we should have done then, at that time, and at that place. That it wasn't is now a waste of time to debate. Does anyone really think that he will recant what he believed then? Why should he, anyway? Let's just admit that he was wrong and let it go at that. The point, of course, is not to live in the past; that territory has long been won over and populated by the neurotics among us. It is best to know about the past so that its injustices will not be repeated, that's all. For if they are repeated, then we only have ourselves to blame for allowing those among us who have no voice, no forum, no means for redress, to be treated with anything less than the respect they deserve.

And no, the Valley is not paradise nor was it meant to be. But then, it wasn't meant to be Hell either, although it was that for many and for many years. And before anyone goes off the deep end in a rhapsody or in rapture of federal governmental laws, to improve our lot or that of any other group, experience and common sense have demonstrated that laws which are not enforced are but words on paper. And so, the Valley, that jurisdictional barrier, is alive and well with love and betrayal, with undying friendships and with un-dying enmities, with racial and class discrimination, with new American citizens and old ones and with all the tensions that make life worth living. After all, without tensions and contradictions, life usually means that someone is in constant control, a situation that guarantees unbridled power and which then provides a feeding ground for the scalping of the helpless.

Just recently, a woman friend sent me a definition of a literary critic which, in many ways, defines any critic who is not involved in a higher service for his fellow citizens; this is what she wrote: "Literary critics are like military observers on a hill watching the carnage below and who, after the battle, come down and slaughter the survivors."

Are we critics or are we participants? In the Valley, there are many critics and few participants, but make no mistake, it has been the participants who have carried the battle on this or on that side of the river.

E PLURIBUS VITAE
(1973)

At one time in his youth and years before I was born, my father was an active revolutionary. He gave of himself, of his time, and much of his own personally hard-earned money to support the Mexican Revolution as well as to support émigrés of all stations who found themselves in the United States. As I mentioned earlier, I did not know him then, of course, for I had not been born. In fact, I didn't know my father until I was four years old when he finally came home to stay. Now, many years later and some twenty-three years after his death, I imagine it must have been a frustrating and trying condition for him to settle down or to stay put as an ordinary townsman.

I do know that although he owned our home and a few lots in and around Mercedes, his earnings and savings went out to other revolutionaries whom he considered less fortunate. Because of this and other acts, we accepted the fact that we had to do without some things. I forget now what they were but, surely, they must have been important then.

All of the preceding is but a bare mention of the many lives led by my father, Don Manuel G. Hinojosa who, in his sixty-five years, also worked as a *peón*, as a gandy dancer, as a shepherd in Wyoming, as a farmer in the Gulf Coastal bend and as a gambler. In another set of lives, he also owned a dairy farm and three dry cleaning shops; he must have certainly had other dealings of which I personally did not know. This information, then, was gleaned, for the most part, subconsciously, as I sat playing on the living room floor when people of all sorts would come to call on him. I learned of his many lives through others, never from him.

I remember playing on our side porch one afternoon when our car appeared suddenly as if by magic. I must have stood on the running board, there being no other way for me to see inside the car. What I saw was a man who had borrowed by father's car to make a business trip or something and, as I stood there, on the running board, I saw that the man was bleeding. Again, as if by magic, people appeared and the man was taken inside our home and, directly, to my father's bedroom. The man recovered and lived with us during his convalescence. In gratitude, he gave me a calf. Later, the man had a falling out with my father; my father never spoke harshly of the man although the man's name would come up in conversations from time to time. A year before my father died, the man came to our home and asked my older brother for permission to see my father. The man removed his hat, walked to my father's bed and offered his hand. We were, all of us, standing there watching a small, solemn event in the life of a man.

My father was also a policeman and by virtue of this authority in a small Valley town, he also served as adviser and counselor to whomever needed help and advice. He gave unstintingly of himself to others, and although we didn't know it at the time, he was showing us still another one of his many lives.

Through reflection and induction and by means of countless conversations among ourselves, the children, we also learned that all of his lives were made possible by our mother who did not stand in his way. A strong, resolute woman, my mother inculcated a love and a respect for him which are still very much a part of our own lives. Her strength, then, went hand in hand with my father's manner of living.

I, too, have lived many lives, although by comparison, they pale and fade away; my lives and the idea of living several lives, however, were made possible, in great part, by his example. All of this came to mind at a party I attended some years ago, and again, recently, at another party. Everyone talked of what they had done at one time or another. I confess that I, too, fell into that trap. It was seldom that anyone talked of what was happening now. That, I discovered again, was the main difference: my father always talked of what was happening now and of what would happen in the future as a consequence. I believe that I've maintained the same outlook as he did.

Now, looking back and forward to my life, I find that I had a happy childhood; for this, I'm grateful, but more so, for his love of life and for the many lives he left me.

BREVE PESQUISA DEL VALLE
DEL RÍO GRANDE
(2000)

L a región del Valle del Río Grande fue la última de las colonias de la corona española; el ejército español empezó la agrimensura en la cuarta década del siglo dieciocho bajo el mando de don José de Escandón. De las cinco partidas, la primera originó desde la capital mexicana, dada su distancia más lejana, luego la de Querétaro, seguida por la de Tampico, Tamaulipas, y por fin, las dos más cercanas a la frontera, las que provinieron de Monterrey, Nuevo León, y de Saltillo, Coahuila, respectivamente.

El primer censo se tomó en 1750, y muchos de los apellidos como Canales, García, Garza, Guerra, Hinojosa, Leal, Treviño, etc. forman parte de los apellidos que aparecieron en el censo original.

Dado que esa región linda con el estado de Tamaulipas, que da frente al golfo mexicano, que su aislamiento del estado de Texas y el país, y que los, originarios y vecinos del lugar aún permanecen en tierra y las mercedes expedidas por la corona, la manutención del idioma español no ha sido tan difícil como en otras partes de Texas o de la parte suroeste de Estados Unidos. Para agregar a esta letanía de circunstancias, sigue siendo una región rural; sabido es que lo rural no tiende a deformar el idioma ni la cultura tan rápidamente como ocurre en lugares urbanizados. A la vez ya que estamos tan cerca, o como aún se oye por allá, ya que estamos juntos con pegados a México, el conservadurismo cultural permanece fuerte y viable. Como las familias aún siguen cruzando de diario los varios puentes internacionales en la región, como hay casamientos hoy igual que antes, las parentelas siguen en marcha. Debido también a esos lazos estrechos, el idioma que se habla en la banda norteña no se ha estancado por completo dada la infusión diaria del idioma español norteño mexicano.

Es, en fin, un lugar *sui géneris*. Distinto, pues, a una Tijuana con su rápida urbanización y su cambio radical no sólo en el número de habitantes sino también en su provenencia en los últimos treinta años, ya que muchos que han llegado a esa parte de Baja California, provienen de otros estados, en particular del sur y del suroeste de México. Esa inestabilidad no quiere decir que Tijuana no sigue siendo territorio mexicano ni mucho menos, pero sí quiere decir que los cambios allí han sido más rápidos y deformantes.

La economía del Valle sigue, en su gran proporción, basada en lo agrícola y eso, la tierra, es lo que ha llegado a cementar una querencia al Valle. Importante también es que esa larga estancia de más de dos siglos y medio en el mismo sitio ha establecido la estabilidad que se necesita para identificarse íntimamente con el lugar.

El número de los diputados federales le corresponden al sur de Texas dado el número de habitantes: cuatro, y los cuatro son méxicotexanos: Ortiz, González, Bonilla e Hinojosa. El Valle cuenta con más de treinta poblados; muchos de ellos a dos o tres millas de distancia de cada uno.

Como tienden a casarse entre sí, de pueblo a pueblo, también tienden a permanecer allí. Así, por un ejemplo, cuando los jóvenes terminan sus estudios universitarios, la gran mayoría vuelve al Valle a trabajar. Existe, pues, una rancia tradición de educarse formalmente. Aún allá, en los tiempos durante la primera guerra mundial cuando el número de méxico-texanos en las escuelas públicas era reducidísimo, el Valle mantenía sus propias estructuras. Ya para 1915, José T. Canales era miembro de la legislatura estatal. Debido al acta de derechos educativos otorgados a los veteranos después de la segunda guerra mundial y las otras guerras y aventuras de este país, los administradores y los profesores en las escuelas públicas son, en su gran mayoría, méxico-texanos. Además, los estudiantes méxico-texanos en las escuelas públicas cuentan con un promedio de noventa y cinco a noventa y siete por ciento. Igual que los administradores, los profesores son, en su gran mayoría, méxico-texanos. Esto no quiere decir que el Valle sea un paraíso, pero sí quiere decir que no somos una minoría.

Lo mismo se ve en la política del lugar. Desde fines de los sesenta, ya no es el caso de que un méxico-texano sea nombrado o seleccionado por los anglo-texanos para que se presente para un puesto u otro. Ya no. Ahora el candidato Alaniz se presenta contra el candidato Salinas, o el candidato Treviño se presenta contra el candidato Ramírez para un puesto u otro. Además, las mujeres del Valle también se presentan como alcaldes, procuradores judiciales, etcétera.

Pues, sí, la larga estancia en un mismo sitio bien puede dar esos resultados, pero tal cosa no hubiera sido factible sin la educación. En el Valle, cuando se fundó en el siglo dieciocho, no se fundaron ni fuertes ni presidios ni iglesias. Se fundaron escuelas. Los pocos sacerdotes que venían no venían a quedarse ni a establecer iglesias; lo más que fundaban eran misiones como la misión Santa Rita o la misión Toluca.

Los indígenas que vivían en la región nunca fueron sujetos a trabajar para la iglesia; unos se quedaron y otros, pasando el tiempo, se mezclaron con los nuevos colonos en ambas bandas del río.

Esa vida duró por cien años; la primera batalla en lo que en inglés se le denomina como The Mexican-American War y que en México se le llama La Guerra del '47, empezó en el Valle en abril de 1846. Esa batalla, que eso es lo que fue y no una escaramuza, da comienzo a esa guerra en la cual México perdió territorio que cubre más millas cuadradas que el México actual. Al ratificarse el Tratado Guadalupe-Hidalgo aquel cuatro de julio de 1848, la gente del Valle vivía tan aislada como antes de la guerra. Esa barrera entre los dos países era y sigue siendo una barrera jurisdiccional que no cultural. El español que hablamos en la banda norteña forma parte del español que se habla en los cuatro estados que lindan con Texas: Tamaulipas, Nuevo León, Coahuila y Chihuahua. Ligado a ambos lados de la frontera aún más; pero las ligaduras viejas también son importantísimas porque son ligaduras psicológicas, comerciales, históricas y culturales.

No fue hasta la guerra civil norteamericana que el Valle sufrió la primera de varias inmigraciones por los ciudadanos norteamericanos, primero por parte de gente del sur y luego los inmigrantes del mesoeste que portaban consigo todo el bagaje de su supuesta superioridad; pero les ocurrió, pasando el tiempo, lo que le ocurre a cualquier ejército de ocupación, sea éste militar o civil. La tercera inmigración ocurrió en los años veinte y ésta fue nociva. Si los primeros inmigrantes vivían a gusto tanto en Tamaulipas o en Texas y aprendieron español y se casaron con hombres y mujeres de ambos lados del río, los inmigrantes de los años veinte poco trataron de asimilarse o de aculturarse como los inmigrantes del siglo diecinueve.

Esos fueron años difíciles para el Valle porque las familias fundadoras ahora se veían discriminadas. Después de la década de los veinte, vino la era de la Gran Depresión ecónomica, seguida por la segunda guerra mundial. Sin embargo, unos diez años después de la guerra, los méxico-texanos empezaron a recobrar el poder, tanto económico como político que, dicho sea en verdad, muchas veces son indistinguibles.

Este empuje por educarse también se debe a la Revolución Mexicana. El clima benigno del Valle, el gran número de hispanoparlantes en esa parte del estado, su proximidad a la frontera y el gran número de gente emparentada con tamaulipecos, potosinos y neoleoneses, hizo del Valle del Río Grande un lugar ideal para los exiliados de la Revolución. Muchos de estos hombres y mujeres se ganaban la vida como profesores en el Valle durante una u otra etapa de la Revolución. Gente letrada fueron ellos los que establecieron las ya citadas "escuelitas" donde uno aprendía a escribir, a leer, la aritmética y donde el día escolar se cerraba con el himno nacional en pleno Estados Unidos al cantar "Mexicanos, al grito de guerra, al sonoro rugir del cañón . . .". Sabíamos que éramos ciudadanos norteamericanos, sin duda alguna, pero también sabíamos que éramos mexicanos. Además, si a uno se le olvidaba lo que era, allí estaban nuestros conciudadanos anglotexanos para hacernos memoria de que no éramos iguales. Pero en este mundo todo se acaba y lo dicho ha pasado a la historia. Con una frontera porosa, con un sistema de apoyo psicológico y de sangre la historia del Valle siempre ha sido y es otra cosa.

Para acabar, en mis clases al empezar el año escolar, suelo preguntarle a los estudiantes no-graduados de dónde provienen. Los de El Paso, o Del Río, o de San Antonio, nombran las ciudades igual que los no-graduados anglo-texanos que dicen que son de Houston, Dallas, Fort Worth o de donde sean.

No así los del Valle; se les pregunta y responden "I'm from the Valley". Yo entonces tengo que preguntarles que de qué pueblo en el Valle, pero, como se dijo, la primera respuesta sempiterna es, "I'm from the Valley", es decir, "Yo soy del Valle".

Eso es saber quién y de dónde es uno.

Para repetir, no es un paraíso ni cosa que lo parezca. La mayoría de las fechorías, los crímenes, el mercado de drogas, los homicidios, etcétera se deben a los méxico-texanos. Pero también hay que recordar que menos del diez por ciento de los habitantes son anglo-texanos.

También hay ciertas consecuencias de criarse en ambiente y una consecuencia es que los padres quieren que sus hijos vuelvan al Valle al recibirse de la universidad. Tales puntos de vista forman parte del apoyo familiar, pero también tienden a achatar la ambición y los planes de las jóvenes. Como saben que soy del Valle, vienen a verme para ver si puedo convencer a los padres. Esto me presenta todo tipo de problemas, ya que difícil es volcar la cultura empedernida.

Pasa que el Valle es nuestra casa, nuestro hogar, y como nos dice Robert Frost, "Home, when you have to go there, is where they have to take you in." "El hogar, cuando tengas que volver a él, es donde tienen que alojarte".

PUENTES
(2001)

Sabido es que los puentes tanto sirven para unir como para separar. En ciertos casos, figuran como lazos para el pasado, el presente y, si siguen en pie, para el futuro. En mi caso, los puentes me interesan, sean ya grandes, chicos, nuevos, viejos o históricos y, en particular, los puentes internacionales. Se debe, quizás a que yo nací cercano a uno y me crié a unos cuantos pasos de otro; ambos en el valle bajo del Río Grande, a unos minutos donde el río desemboca en el golfo mexicano.

El de mi niñez ligaba Thayer, Texas, con Río Rico, Tamaulipas. Los dos sitios han desaparecido: víctimas de una inundación en los años cuarenta. Pero la influencia de cruzar ese puente con mi padre vive en la memoria y en la imaginación. Se mezclan, pues, igual que la gente que vive en ambos lados del puente.

También pasa que lo que me fascina de los puentes es que al cruzar de un lado al otro, uno parece caer en otro mundo. Pero esto es una mera apariencia. En la realidad de las cosas, un efecto de los puentes internacionales es la formación y conjunción de dos culturas que, a la vez, dan vida a una cultura *sui géneris.*

Si un norteamericano monolingüe, pongamos por caso, cruza de Irún a Hendaya, verá dos países, oirá dos idiomas y, para su pobre fortuna, creerá que presencia dos culturas cuando, en efecto, se encuentra en medio de dos culturas que producen su propia cultura que forma parte de la mentalidad fronteriza.

Otra cosa en común entre la gente fronteriza es que la gente de las fronteras piensa más en sí y en los del otro lado del puente que en sus conciudadanos que viven en el interior de sus respectivos países. Como digo, es una cultura *sui géneris*: parte de una cultura, parte de otra, y por fin, su propia cultura.

A veces, dado a los procesos históricos, los países más cercanos han guerreado entre sí, pero sé de buena tinta que alguien de Kehl tiene más en común con alguien de Estrasburgo que con alguien de Colonia o de Berlín. Así como alguien de Lorena tiene más que ver con el lindante estado alemán que con París o Normandía. Esto es de lo más natural, ya que comparten los mismos espacios históricos, psicológicos, comerciales, geográficos y culturales.

Todo esto sin mencionar la mezcla de sangres que ocurre frecuentemente entre la gente fronteriza. Por decirlo en paráfrasis a Quevedo, los lazos de la parentela estiran más que una carreta.

En el teje y maneje de un lado y el otro, se ve que los idiomas cambian con más frecuencia, que la gente se ajusta más fácilmente y, casi sin querer, esto produce una mentalidad de autosuficiencia.

Que nosotros los profesores y estudiosos reneguemos, con o sin razón, no forma parte de este corto ensayo. Lo que sí se puede asegurar es que la autosuficiencia, a su vez, produce una autosatisfacción y los fronterizos quedan muy seguros de sí mismos.

En mi caso, aislados como estábamos de Washington, D.C. y de la capital mexicana, uno era de "este lado" o "del otro lado" y con eso bastaba para identificarse. De ahí las preguntas sempiternas: ¿Quiénes son tus padres? ¿Tus parientes? ¿Dónde naciste?

En fin, preguntas para cerciorar si uno era de ese lugar o si uno era un "fuereño", como aún se dice en mi suelo natal.

En las fronteras el lugar de origen es más que importante. Es, en una palabra, esencial, ya que con la información preliminar, se empieza a desenlazar la cuerda de la procedencia de la persona. Esto parece como si fuera cosa de gente rural, pero no. Cruce usted los puentes Stanton o Santa Fe en las ciudades gemelas de El Paso, Texas, y Ciudad Juárez, Chihuahua, con sus dos millones y medio, lo primero que se pregunta es querer saber no solamente quién es quién, sino, lo esencial, de quién. Establecido lo susodicho, los que hablan llegan a un acuerdo tocante el idioma que van a usar en esa instancia. Lo inevitable es que en unos cuantos minutos, se mezclan los dos idiomas.

No hablo aquí de esnobs, ya que esa pobre gente tiene otras preocupaciones no siempre ligadas a la vida actual, es decir, al teje y meneje mencionado.

Lo que se debe aceptar, quieran o no, es que la cultura fronteriza es parte de la vida cotidiana, y por consiguiente se vive sin pedirle permiso a nadie.

Es un hecho de esa vida particular donde los puentes abarcan los dos lados. El cruce, en mi caso, entre Texas y los cuatro estados mexicanos (Tamaulipas, Nuevo León, Coahuila y Chihuahua) es de lo más fácil, ya que esa frontera es bastante porosa. Para acabar, no todos los que cruzan son ilegales. A veces, los "de este lado" nadan y lo cruzan solamente para saludar o para visitar a sus parientes "del otro lado". En estos casos, la frontera méxico-estadounidense actúa como barrera jurisdiccional pero no como barrera cultural.

Esto también es algo que ocurre a diario en las fronteras que, de un modo u otro, no siempre son infranqueables.

DE NOCHE TODOS LOS INMIGRANTES SON PARDOS, CON EXCEPCIONES (2007)

L a actual revolución social y económica en Estados Unidos tiene muchas ramas y todas tienen que ver con lo rico que es este país, con lo mal gobernado que está este país que, en efecto, es más bien un continente. ¿Cómo, pues, gobernar, aclarar, dirigir o, a lo menos, establecer una política que produja ideas y planes que concuerden con los gustos y las nececidades económicas de cincuenta estados? Bien puede ser que sea una imposibilidad pero, como en todo, lo mejor es sentarse y entablar conversaciones. El único que sepa si esta sugerencia sa va a llevar a cabo es Dios y Él mismo sabe que el que esto escribe tiene pocas esperanzas que algo de beneficio (para todos) se logre. Llámenle pesimismo si quieren pero lo que es, hablando en plata esterlina, es una realidad tan grande como una casa, la Blanca si se empeñan.

Por consiguiente, ya que los monolingües en los múltiples campos gubernamentales no van a entender, y deje usted de entender, de comprender lo que sigue, puede servir para dar reparo a cualquiera. Voy a hablar de las excepciones, de gente que, sin ser culpables, tuvo que abandonar su país, sus empleos, casas, propiedades, parientes, para que sus hijos tuvieran la oportunidad de vivir más o menos tranquilamente y que tuvieran la oportunidad de ser productivos en el país al cual se mudaron para lograr esa oportunidad. Empiezo con un salto atrás, la Revolución Mexicana a principios del siglo 20.

Esta guerra, como todas, fue horrible y produjo todo tipo de trastorno interno tanto en México como en Estados Unidos, el país que salió ganando hombres y mujeres que formaron gran parte de la capa laboral que ayudó a este país a ensancharse hasta rivalizar al imperio británico en poder territorial, económico, militar y político.

El desastre económico que empezó en octubre del '29, presenció un desmoronamiento social mundialmente; este país sufrió una dislocación, un desganche moral en el sentido de que familias se separaron, se mudaron a diversas partes del país, y muchas pasaron hambre. Para los de la actual generación, bien pueden acudir a cualquier biblioteca para ver fotos de hombres sin trabajo haciendo cola para comer algo, cualquier cosa, ya que no encontraban empleo porque no lo había. Una verdad tan dura y duradera como el granito.

Diecinueve años antes, en 1910, estalla la Revolución Mexicana, suceso, dada la proximidad de México y Estados Unidos, que vio la dislocación del país vecino. Y tanta fue la dislocación y de tal envergadura que benefició a Estados Unidos al abrir las puertas a gente trabajadora y de talento en diversos campos.

En este ensayo me he de enfocar en la familia de don José García que había sido profesor en una escuela pública en uno de los pueblos tamaulipecos no lejos de la frontera. Su mujer, doña Faustinita, era ama de casa aunque también educada como su esposo. Cruzaron el río y se asentaron en Mercedes, Texas. Lo que sigue fue lo que realizó esta familia al emigrar a este país. De paso, breve mención se hará de don Abel, hermano menor de don José.

Con muy escasos recursos, los chicos se pusieron a trabajar y a educarse en las escuelas públicas en Mercedes. El mayor, José

Antonio, al recibirse de la secundaria, se marchó a Austin, encontró trabajo y se inscribió en la Universidad de Texas. Así que se recibió, hizo aplicación a la escuela de medicina de Galveston, se le aceptó y se recibió como médico. Siguiéndole la pauta, su hermano, Héctor hizo lo mismo. Me detengo aquí para hacerles memoria de que la discriminación racial en Texas seguía firme. Al recibirse, Héctor se mudó a Corpus Christi para ejercer su profesión. Estalla la llamada segunda guerra mundial, se da de alta, y sirve como médico en África y luego en Italia. Viene la paz pero la discriminación no ha disminuido en el estado. Para combatirla, Héctor Pérez García forma y establece el American G.I. Forum, así como dar un día por semana a la gente necesitada de Corpus Christi. La historia del G.I. Forum es bien conocida por los historiadores; una de sus primeras batallas fue el escándalo en el villorio de Three Rivers, Texas, donde no se permitió que se efectuara el velorio de Félix Longoria, veterano que había caído en Europa, en la propiedad de la casa mortuoria.

El doctor García intercede, llama al senador Lyndon B. Johnson y le explica lo ocurrido. En fin, la casa murtuoria cede pero tarde, ya que el senador Johnson, a petición del doctor García y de la familia Longoria, lograron que el entierro se hiciera en el cementerio militar en Arlington, Virginia. Este caso y el talento organizador del doctor García causó que se establecieran organizaciones del American G.I. Forum en diversos estados para la protección política y social de los méxico-americanos.

Mientras tanto, José Antonio se presentó como candidato al concilio educativo de las escuelas públicas en Corpus Christi, donde sirvió por largos años hasta su muerte; en reconocimiento el concilio dedicó una escuela primaria en su nombre.

Cleotilde tambien trabajó como sus hermanos para ganar su diploma en la Universidad de Texas. Se dedicó a la enseñanza por unos años, ahorró su dinero y también se recibió como médico en Galveston. Ella también se mudó a Corpus Christi, dando servicios médicos un día de cada semana para la gente necesitada. Activa políticamente, sirvió en el concilio Del Mar College por muchos años y publicó varios libros. Un estudio trata el descubrimiento por Alonso de Piñeda del Río de las Palmas en 1521. A ese río internacional ahora se le llama el Río Bravo y el Río Grande. También publicó textos de historia sobre la historia de Texas.

Su hijo, Antonio, se recibió como abogado y prestó sus servicios como abogado federal en el distrito sureño de Texas.

El que siguió, Cuauhtémoc, también se inscribió en Austin pero murió en su juventud mientras hacía sus estudios. A él le siguieron Cuitláhuac que también se recibió como médico, y el menor de los hombres, Xicoténcatl, que hizo lo mismo. Cuítlahuac y su mujer, enfermera, se establecieron en San Antonio y sus hijos también se dedicaron a la medicina. La hija de Xicoténcatl hizo sus estudios en Southern Methodist University en Comunicación y se le otorgó un premio nacional por su programa sobre la SIDA, el cual se premió por la Public Broadcasting Service.

La menor de las hermanas García, Dalia, después de su carrera universitaria, se dedicó a dirigir el despacho de su hermana y proveer un programa de caridad en Corpus Christi.

Cabe decir que cada uno de los García realizó los estudios universitarios de por sí, es decir, sin ayuda de los otros hermanos; no es que no querían o que no necesitaban la ayuda económica sino que todos, empezando con José Antonio, el mayor, vieron sus carreras como un reto tal y como los padres lo habían propuesto. La independencia y el coraje necesario es evidente en cada uno de estos hijos de emigrantes.

Por lo que toca a don Abel, hermano menor de don José, sus tres hijos, como veteranos, recibieron sus grados universitarios bajo el programa conocido popularmente como el G.I. Bill. Antonio, el mayor, se dedicó a la abogacía y sirvió en la cámara de diputados en Austin. Abel chico se encargó de la tienda establecida por sus tíos y Amado se dedicó a la enseñanza y cada verano acompañaba a familias migrantes al mesoeste del país para impartir clases a los chicos bajo un programa federal. El menor, Amador, después de su servicio militar y de sus estudios universitarios, estableció su gabinete como abogado en Corpus Christi; a mí me tocó ser profesor de su hija mientras ella cursaba sus estudios en la Universidad de Texas.

Hay más, pero esto no es un estudio a fondo sino un reconocimiento de una familia que sirvió como ejemplo para muchos méxico-americanos en esa parte de Texas, y en el caso de Héctor, que después de su servicio como embajador en las Naciones Unidas, continuó su vida ayudando a los más necesitados a educarse.

Desgraciadamente, para los periódicos y en la mente y percepción del público en general, los inmigrantes son gente nociva. Se equivocan ya que en su gran mayoría, los inmigrantes son gente trabajadora y empecinada en trabajar en lo que pueda para proveer oportunidades a sus hijos.

Sí, vidas ejemplares las de los García, pero seguramente debe haber muchos otros casos parecidos de emigrantes que, por su servicio, tanto al país como a la comunidad, han trabajado y siguen trabajando para el mejoramiento propio y del prójimo.

NI CON GASOLINA

(2008)

El racismo en mi Texas no se quita ni con gasolina; está tan arraigado y tan difícil de extirpar como los pobres que, según el Buen Libro, siempre estarán con nosotros. Y, como en nuestro país hay mucho de donde escoger, los judíos se presentaron como unos de los primeros y luego ferozmente los irlandeses, pero, con excepción de algunas capas sociales, esto ya pasó. De los nuevos estadounidenses, los asiáticos también sufren aunque en la mayoría de los casos, silenciosamente.

Donde no ha desaparecido ha sido contra los negros y nosotros; aquí no trato de los cubanos ya que a ellos también se les increpa por mayoreo en muchas secciones de Miami y sus alrededores.

¿A quiénes se les debe este encono, este odio, este menosprecio? A los hombres, en su gran mayoría; ¿las mujeres? Sí, pero es pobre el número si se compara con los varones. Risible es y como para caerse de espaldas cuando un señor racista macizo es padre de unas hijas de bien ver que de repente se enamoran de dos de la raza y no solo eso sino que se casan con ellas. Y si las chicas son de tezón, como estas dos de quienes hablo, el padre tiene que aguantarse ya que lo susodicho pasó hace treinta años en mi Mercedes.

Los que poco me conocen dirán (entre sí) pero tú, Rolando, tu madre era bolilla. Bien dicho, pero para eso hay que recurrir a la historia: mi madre, Carrie Smith Phillips, nació en 1887 y se crió entre raza en el rancho Galveston y todos mis tíos y tías aprendieron y hablaron español. Es decir, antes de que llegaran las parvadas en los años veinte del siglo veinte ya que esa pobre gente trajo consigo (y qué bagaje, señor don Simón) creyéndose superiores y allí que empezó el racismo en el Valle. En los otros pueblos alemanes en el centro de Texas (New Braunfels, Niederwald, Schulenberg, Rosenberg, Weimar, New Ulm, Fredericksburg, Gruene, etc.) el racismo ya les venía de abolengo. ¿Y perjudicaba? Sí. En New Braunfels, solo un ejemplo, la raza no podía asistir arriba del quinto año en las escuelas públicas.

Pero esto ha cambiado igual que en Seguín y en otros pueblos alemanes en esta parte de Texas; donde sigue el racismo es en Fredericksburg y Kerrville, pero eso también cambiará. Pero no por la benevolencia de leyes federales sino porque andando el tiempo, la raza se educa y actúa.

No hay que creerse que en el Valle no lo había, y debe aclararse que empezó en los veinte; por ejemplo, en Edcouch —pueblo nuevo en el Valle— donde llegaron alemanes, *malgré nous*, en los veinte y pasaron una ley que los *Spanish* y los *Mexicans* (así y sin rodeos) no podían vivir ni entrar y que a los únicos que dejaban entrar eran las criadas y los jardineros que después, al bajar el sol, volvían a La Villa o a donde fuera.

Una mala ley, sí. ¿Y qué le pasa a las malas leyes? Se desmoronan dándole tiempo al tiempo ya que el número de raza en Edcouch actualmente cuenta con ochenta y siete por ciento.

Pero como los que me conocen saben, digo y repito que el Valle no es un paraíso. Muchas de las albercas estaban vedadas, y en Mission, durante la depresión de los treinta y aunque el dinero escaseaba se propuso una escuela secundaria para la raza. No llegó a nada, pero no hay que olvidar que se propuso.

Pero sí hubo raza que sufrió y que leyó anuncios en restoranes que rezaban "No Mexicans or Dogs Allowed" y otros insultos nada sutiles en Edna, Refugio, Victoria y otros pueblos. Y ya que estamos con pueblos y ciudades y regiones que la pasaron peor, allí están San Angelo, Snyder, Midland y Odessa, y otros pueblos de West Texas y hasta ahora, en el presente, El Paso.

Lo escrito es bien poco y se escribe para que los jóvenes tengan cuidado, que recuerden que no todo el monte es de orégano, que hay que ser vigilantes y no dejar pasar los insultos, los menosprecios, sino enfrentarlos.

Para acabar, durante mis años estudiantiles en Austin, había tres de habla hispana en la facultad: don Carlos Castañeda, del Valle y el doctor George I. Sánchez, neo-mexicano que, con el doctor Herschel Manuel, la hicieron de padrinos y originadores de la educación bilingüe antes de que el término existiera. ¿El tercero? Un señor que no conocí de apellido Villarreal quien, según mi pariente Américo Paredes, pronunciaba su nombre Veeyay Real. Éstos tampoco han desaparecido.

CROSSING THE LINE
THE CONSTRUCTION OF A POEM
(1977)

I n the Fall of 1977, my first Fall quarter in Minnesota, I found myself unable to get started on a piece about the Korean War. This was a subject which had been on my mind since the early spring of that same year, when I had managed to write one brief poem called "Native Son Home From Asia" which the poet Alurista published in his journal, *Maize* (I, 3). But that was all I had managed to set down. I was stuck; there *it* was, and here I was with little else to show for it. Still, I thought something was there nibbling and nibbling away, although unable to crack the shell.

I then decided to do what I do best: read. I find that reading solves several problems for me: I'm busy and therefore there's no guilt feeling that comes from inactivity, it also keeps me off the streets, and, as is usually the case, I learn something else about myself. I was sure, I told myself, that something would crop up.

I read some seven or eight histories on the War, and upon finishing them, I discovered to my delight that, invariably, the historians, military and civilians alike, had made shameless use of U.S. Army Public Information releases and other handouts. Among this welter, there was a curious book, a little one, written by a field grade officer in the Indian Army who had been there as an observer. The book concerned itself, primarily, with problems of logistics, and, secondarily, with the tactics and strategy employed by both sides. Also, it did contain a reliable table on chronology. After all of that reading, what I had on my hands were what one would expect: some mental and some handwritten notes that made little sense once removed from the context of the reading.

Now, a writer, this writer, enters easily enough into a state of self-delusion about something being there ready to come out and to be written, but even self-delusion can be carried only so far, and when reality rushes in one has to accept certain facts. One may not wish to believe those facts, but Budgell* certainly knew what he was talking about when he wrote that matters of fact are very stubborn things which refuse to go away. In my case, the facts were that, although I may have had something in mind, I had nothing to write about for the time being.

I decided to read some more; I reread Anthony Powell's *Dance to the Music of Time,* as well as some of his earlier works (1905-2000); after this, I wrote down some names, but this didn't work, and, added to which, I then had to admit that I had no story to tell. All I had was a suspicion that something was brewing. With that suspicion, and little else, I decided to write some lines in Spanish with an idea of translating them into English. The result of this piece of business was that one set of lines was as bad as the other. In brief, then, five months were spent writing from late Spring to early Fall with precious little to show for it. On the other hand, I was enjoying my classes that fall of '77, exploring the new surroundings in Minnesota, and I was also thinking on the two inches of snow which had fallen in a matter of a few hours on the eighth of October, and, as usual, wondering when I was ever going to write again.

I then took to getting around campus and meeting some of my colleagues in the departments of English, Spanish and Portuguese and in the American Studies Program, all within the College of

---

*Eustace Budgell, English author, 1686-1737.

Liberal Arts. This was all very well and to the good, as you may imagine, but the writing wasn't getting done. As I said earlier, Budgell was right: the fact was I couldn't write anything at the time. But writers, if anything, are just as stubborn as facts.

I then read a chapter of a novel I had been working on for some two or three years; as you can see, I was reduced to reading my own stuff in order to see if there were something there to unlock the dam, open the locks, etcetera. The section I mention is called "Con el pie en el estribo," and it appeared in *The Bilingual Review/La Revista Bilingüe* (III, 1). I read it aloud; I then recorded it on a cassette and listened to it. But this too bore no fruit as far as I could tell.

This state of affairs can produce what the late Walt Kelly, the creator of *Pogo*, once called "the joe blakes." Now, one of the consequences of the Joe blakes' is constant worry, another is frustration, and this, at times, can lead to the kicking of an otherwise innocent household cats of which we have three. One serious result of cat kicking is that it tends to strain family relations, to say nothing of the cat's feelings and future attitude and relationship.

At this time I should like to confess that I believe in Christmas and in Christmas gifts. A few days before Christmas in that Fall quarter of 1977, a line in English, not in prose exactly, but in rhythm, as an attempt at poetry, came from somewhere: "At Harvey Lann's Hardware Store, Margaret wants to know." It came after some rewriting, but it came, nonetheless. Now, in Spanish prosody, a twelve-syllable verse is the usual line form of the *arte mayor*. The *arte mayor* is an old, reliable eight-verse, twelve-syllable form; it was muscled out of Spanish letters at the beginning of the sixteenth century by the newer Italian hepta and hendecasyllabic lines which had been introduced to the Peninsula, we are told, by Juan Boscán Almogárer, among others; it is written down that Boscán himself had been introduced to this new rhythm by Andrea Navaggiero, the Italian man of letters and politics. The *arte mayor* didn't die, of course, it was merely laid aside like the fourteen-syllable (Spanish, not French) Alexandrine which the *arte mayor* itself had displaced. Rubén Darío, as we all recognize, was to resuscitate both forms three hundred years later for many of us to enjoy.

So, there it was, that first line: "At Harvey Lann's Hardware Store, Margaret wants to know." Counting syllables as is commonly done in Spanish, and as is also done in some contemporary poetry written in English, I decided to follow Spanish prosody although using the English language. Of more importance to me at that moment, of course, was that I had written something that promised some possibilities. The next line came easily enough; it was in the seven syllabic manner: "Whatever did he mean, Harv?" This was followed by: "When I asked Rogelio how it was he spoke that Asian tongue" and then: "He replied that it was due to misspent youth."

I then stopped and asked myself the following question: "Who's Harvey?" I then came up with a much better question: "Who's Margaret?" I say a better question because, after all, it was this woman, this Margaret, who wanted to know something, to resolve something. As to the relationship between these two characters, Margaret, to me, obviously enough, I thought, was Harv's wife. This led to at least two more questions: "What about their relationship, and what is it that she wants to know?"

Looking over the first pencil copy I found that it reads like this: A.

Original and rewrites:

~~Harvey Lann's~~

~~Moodys~~

At Harvey Lann's Hardware Store,

wants to know:

Margaret ~~asks her husband:~~

Whatever did he mean, Harv?

David   Chinese

When I asked ~~Rogelio~~ how it was he spoke ~~that Asian tongue~~

or whatever it is

~~and~~   a product of

~~He~~ replied that it was ~~due to~~ misspent youth.

  ^   ^

he

> At Harvey Lann's Hardware Store, Margaret wants to know:
> Whatever did he mean, Harv? When I asked David how it
> was
> He spoke Chinese
> Or whatever it is,
> He replied that it was a product of misspent youth.

You probably noticed that Rogelio's name was changed to David; later on we'll see why and how this came about and what it led to.

By way of the first of two parenthetical remarks, I should say that I held on to "Crossing the Line" for over two years before I finally sent it off to Nicolás Kanellos at the University of Houston; the poem appeared in *Revista Chicano-Riqueña* VII, 4, p. 6.

The next section was also the result of several rewrites, and it was here that the words *harmless* and *cheap* appeared, were stricken, and reappeared only to be written out again; as can be seen, they finally stuck. It may be that the idea first arose here with *harmless* and *cheap* for the ironic ending in the poem. Irony, as is well known, is the one good defense of the defenseless.

I should now like to mention, briefly, a matter of style. Since Harvey was now going to participate, through speech, I wanted his talk, his speech patterns, to sound like *talk;* nothing new in this, to be sure, but I am sure we'll agree how often some writers forget to make talk sound like talk:

B.

Original and rewrites:

The

~~That~~ boy's not right in the head, Maggie, that's all.

~~does~~

~~and he's willin'~~   ~~and he comes cheap~~

He's strong enough, ~~all right but he's off~~

   ~~he's off, but he's harmless, and he does come cheap~~

~~Harmless, but off~~

                    And
                     ∧
~~and he's harmless.~~ ~~And~~ God knows he's willing

                    ~~and~~

          just

          But it happens that he's
                    ∧
~~Don't He's~~ off a bit. ~~but~~ he's harmless . . . Cheap, too
                    ∧
                   But

Final version:
The boy's not right in the head, Maggie, that's all.
   He's strong, And God knows he's willing, but it just happens
That he's off a bit. But he's harmless. . . Cheap, too.

   This is an attempt at natural speech, but, at the same time, I
also wanted to have Harvey introduce himself by means of his own
selection of words. What we have here, then, is a broad
brush-stroke description of the boy reduced to his being harmless,
cheap, strong, willing and off a bit, but harmless. This, of course,
is to reassure Margaret that she's safe. And this, as you can see, is
also Harvey's point of view; we still have to hear from Margaret
and from the boy's side of it. Still, it was a description, and Harvey, at this point, thinks he has answered Margaret's question to
her satisfaction. The chances are very good that you are way ahead
of me here: they're talking at cross purposes, and you're right.
   I was now in the middle of a poem coming out in English and
using Spanish prosody as I fluctuated between eleven and thirteen
syllables to carry it out; sometimes a line of seven syllables would
be followed by a line of five or, to break the monotony that could
set in, a long verse of fourteen would be followed by another long

verse and thus allow the work itself to find its proper rhythm as I chose one word or this word over another or that one and so on. A poem written in English using Spanish syllabic norms.

Partially satisfied with the first rewrite of that first part which introduces the characters, Margaret's question was still unresolved, and I wasn't sure as to who these people were. The last thing I wanted was to allow the reader to be kept completely in the dark. This is an important consideration; of equal importance was that the way the poem was laid out so far, the piece itself cried out for more information: "Who are these people?"

Obviously, I thought, the time had come to somehow round out the Lanns and the young man:

C.

Original and rewrites:

crossed over

Harvey's a shade over fifty; Margaret has ~~just arrived,~~

and it's Saturday nights for them, usually.

Yes, Margaret has just arrived at fifty and

though

and she's sending signals to Harv

finds herself

~~but~~ he's not catching, so Margaret slams drawers full of nails

a bit ~~louder~~ than necessary

firmer

She also

~~Margaret~~ wondered through the day

and through most of the night,

~~was is~~

what it is to make love to a someone who's not quite

~~it~~

right in the head;

to

~~To~~ someone who says 'misspent youth' ~~and 'unconventional as it may seem'~~

and, 'you're in great shape Margaret-girl'

When Harvey's not around

~~and~~

Final version:

> Harvey's a shade over fifty; Margaret has just crossed the line,
> And now it's down to occasional Saturday nights for them.
> Yes, Margaret has just arrived at fifty, and though
> She's sending signals to Harv,
> He's not catching. So,
> Margaret finds herself slamming drawers a bit firmer than
> necessary.
> She also wonders during the day and through the night,
> What it would be like,
> As she says,
> To make love with someone who's not quite right in the head:
> With someone who says, 'Misspent youth' and,
> When Harv's not around: 'You're in great shape, Margaret-
> girl.'

From this we now know of Margaret and Harvey and something about the boy as well as some actions on the part of all three. Margaret's frustration is taken out on the nail drawers, but it would have defeated the tone of the poem to have stated that she was frustrated, since it is recognized that it is far better to show than to tell; and, I prefer to show through those slight gestures or movements, those telltale actions that reveal some inner secret. She's had the occasional Saturday nights, and, just perhaps, she's up to here with Harv, with the hardware store, with having reached fifty. Actually speaking, Margaret has gone through two-thirds of her life already, but has she lived them? Her original question is no longer "Whatever did he mean, Harv?" which, one, is perhaps a half-hearted attempt at confessing that she's noticing the boy, and, two, that Harv is not—has not, continues not—to look at *her*. Something, then, has to happen. The writer has stepped in and promised something, now he has to deliver.

It did not escape me that the characterization was schematic, but I decided that it was enough for now and it was there for us to see: the couple's middle age, their marriage life partially gone to seed, their indifferent sex life, from Margaret's point of view, and a hint of those broad-shouldered little slabs Frost wrote about, as well as the additional information that 1) she daydreams about the boy, and 2) that the boy (harmless as he may seem) is a bit of a predator, and he may know more than he allows. This section also develops and moves the poem along; it informs the reader some more by pointing to Margaret's humanity, to let the reader focus a sympathetic-perhaps an understanding—eye upon Margaret standing there with all that hardware looking gloomily and unhappily at the half-century mark. And then there's the repetition of time that runs across the sense of need, of urgency on Margaret's part.

There's more, of course, the hidden rhyme of *though* and so, and *night/like/quite/right*, and the alliterative */she's sending signals/* and then */during the day/through the night/* which help in keeping a light tone to the poem. There will be no blood spilled, or so one feels from the poem's tone and rhythm.

I was now at the halfway point and as usual trying to follow Ralph Waldon Emerson's precept of "the force of few words." I was determined to tell the story in as few words as possible with the thought of adding strength through brevity, taking care not to be too brief and too obscure, but then not giving the game away either.

At this time, I should add, I was still bothered by Rogelio's identity; I couldn't imagine his demeanor, his face or his height.

For some reason I decided to name him David; I have several characters named David; one of them is David *el tío* who was killed in Korea. This new David turned out to be David Ruiz-Sonny, also a Korean War veteran who had appeared briefly somewhere else. And here's the second parenthetical remark: the Korean theme was dying very hard, and later on in *Korean Love Songs* he was to play an important part.

Well now, I had a Korean War veteran on my hands, and to use a term from The Great War, one who was shell-shocked. This condition may be inferred from Harvey's comment that "the boy's not right in the head." But was he not right in the head? We've seen that the boy takes care to see that Harv's not around when he says what he says to Margaret. For him to say those things could lead one to believe that if Margaret does not encourage him, she neither dissuades nor discourages him, it would seem.

D.

Original and rewrites:

                                             ⟶ was an accessory

                                              to the cat's ~~death~~

                                                   demise

~~It's only a matter of time~~ Curiosity, after all ~~did the cat in~~

and Margaret⟍   ⟍no longer youthful⟍   ⟍wants to know

Wants to know

For Herself.

    h

    David   there placed

~~Rogelio,~~ Harv wants those kegs nearer the door.

When that's done, I'll give you a glass of ice-cold lemonade.

It's a   ~~really~~

∧
~~A~~ substitute that neither one wants

But arranging these things takes time

~~Takes time,~~

                                        has
                                        ∧
and time is something Margaret ~~doesn't have~~

And, yet, doesn't have.

It'll have to be next week, then.

                          ⟋at the general meeting of the
Harv'll be ~~gone to the~~ Belken County Hardware
Distributors Association,

And

~~&~~ I'll have myself a headache, she says.

And she does.

Curiosity doesn't always win out, and thus the cat survives,

        ~~thus~~

~~and the cat need not die;~~

In time,

~~and so,~~ the drawer slamming stops,

                    Saturday

She passes on the nights

~~The Saturdays~~   ~~pass,~~

                                    he's
                                    ↓
and Harv has no complaints about the boy; ~~who's~~ strong,
he works hard

~~he~~   and, ~~he comes~~

~~and works hard~~   ~~Cheap too. And cheap enough.~~

~~most of all, he's harmless & reliable.~~   Cheap, too.

he's ↗reliable.

Final version:

Curiosity, after all, was an accessory to the cat's demise,
and Margaret, no longer youthful,
Wants to know,
for herself.

David, Harv wants those kegs there placed nearer the door.
When that's done, I'll give you a glass of ice-cold lemonade.

It's a substitute that neither one wants, but arranging these things
Takes time, and time is something that Margaret has
And, yet, doesn't have. It'll have to be next week, then.

Harv'll be at the General Meeting of the Belken County
Hardware Distributors,
And I'll have myself a headache, she says.

And she does.

Curiosity doesn't always win, and thus the cat survives.
In time, the drawer slamming stops,
She passes on the occasional Saturday nights,
and Harv has no complaints about the boy; he's strong, he
works hard,
And he's reliable.
Cheap, too.

On the mechanical side of this piece, again, one can see that
the various rewritings affected and produced any number of
idiomatic, rhythmic and syntactical changes.

The tone, a light one, had to be maintained, and the idiosyncratic vision had to be maintained also in order not to jar the reader with any unnecessary surprises.

In regard to Margaret, she is Margaret Lann, a character in a poem and she's rather like many men and women who consider themselves attractive and who wish to be, to remain, sexually active, and failing that, to be noticed. To be seen. Not to be taken for granted; another piece of hardware, as it were. Margaret is very human: she's susceptible to flattery. She's fighting the inevitable pull of gravity that will weigh all of us down to the grave. She is what most of us are: ordinarily and extraordinarily human.

Harv is another matter; he's the proprietor of a small business, a husband, a taxpayer like the rest of us, but he is also something else that many of us are not: he's a cuckold. He isn't a ridiculous figure and no evidence is given that he's foolish. What he is, then, is there, much like David is there. Being there, for some things in life, may mean sadness or pleasure by accident of circumstance, may mean glory or ignominy through unknown or, at times, through mistaken actions, and so forth. We know nothing of the other Harvey Lann, the one he knows, but then he's not under scrutiny here; it's Margaret we're after, and it won't do to dilute a short piece by having too many people in it.

As for David, again, he was there. An object much like the nail drawers, close at hand; an object to be used, and who was used; not necessarily seduced nor the seducer, but used all the same.

In short, what happened to those three in the brief encounter has occurred in many lives throughout history as to be extraordinarily common, that is to say, commonly human.

It's a brief piece, "Crossing the Line," and it isn't—wasn't—meant to be more than that. What it did for me, however, was to begin the writing of *Korean Love Songs* which had been waiting to come in or to get out, depending on one's point of view. "Crossing the Line" led to David, who then led to *Korean Love Songs,* which then led to *Mi querido Rafa / Dear Rafe,* a novel in two parts; the first an epistolary and the second, a reportage. But that's another story.

'50s AUSTIN: A VARIFORM EDUCATION
(2007)

T wo weeks after my honorable discharge after a three-year
sentence defending the country from the evils of Commu-
nism, I drove to the Hidalgo County Courthouse to meet with the
Veterans Affairs adviser. The rumor was he was actor James Stew-
art's father (something he didn't deny), but I was as unconvinced
then as I am today.

A nice enough man, though, and I told him of my plans to
attend The University of Texas. An older brother, René (Class of
'50), attended the University and I visited him and other Valley
friends during my one furlough home; the Army gives one two-
and-a-half days of furlough time for every month served (that's
thirty days a year), and I was planning ahead; the Cold War plan-
ners had other ideas, but that's another story. So, I enrolled and put
in for Cliff Courts as my place of residence. Cliff Courts must have
been leveled over forty years ago and in their place is a gigantic
parking lot just south of Jester dormitory; named for Beauford, a
member of the Board of Regents during the building of the Tower

74   *Rolando Hinojosa*

and later a popular governor who died in office and in harness and was thus succeeded by a wise man: Allen Shivers. Wise because he married one of the Shary women, a native of the Valley, and a Catholic; Shivers was an East Texas Baptist and thus the two largest denominations in the state ganged up to reelect him for life, if he chose.

He also named my brother-in-law's brother as a district judge after my brother-in-law, O. B., turned down the job. Governor Shivers was a year behind O. B. and H. A. García at Pearce Hall, the old law school building. It too has disappeared to be replaced by the current one for which the then U.S. Attorney General, Herbert K. Brownell, delivered the inaugural address.

During my delay en route overseas, I went home for a few days and visited my brother at the university. He lived on 26th and Guadalupe at the Alhambra, aka the H(ispanic) A(merican) House. A good-sized bunch of us, all Valley boys, went to Sixth Street, then a wild and wooly place, some phrase that. I remember one bar in particular, the Hong Kong, which reminded me of some bars I'd been to after basic training. The Hong Kong, of course, is a million lightyears away from the current Sixth Street, a source of pride to many Austinites and well-attended by Baylor students who brave the two-hundred mile round trip on occasion. That part of Sixth Street, obviously, was the Texas Mexican section, but not far from my favorite men's stores: Scarborough's, Merritt, Schaeffer, Brown and Reynolds Penland. Stores which today would go into immediate bankruptcy considering the attire of our current undergraduates, many of whom major in conspicuous poverty.

After my discharge and subsequent enrollment, I took the normal sixteen hours (and, yes, I also worked as did and do many UTers), but sixteen hours, (counting the hour lab) and four years were, in those halcyon days, the number of years one took to graduate although some of us finished in three and, in my case, three-and-a-half; I loved electives and took as many as I could. I worked at the Reserved Reading Room (which is now the Admissions Office) and it stands facing the Registrar's Office, which has always stood on the extreme east of the Tower's rotunda, as it was called, incorrectly, too, since it isn't a rotunda at all; there's norhing round about it unless one considers the runaround one can expect with bureaucracies, no matter how efficient they may be.

Working at the Reading Room (jammed with master's theses and doctoral dissertations, as UT calls its doctoral theses) was the one and only job I held and held on to it dearly; three reasons: I was born into a family of readers and the main library was in the Tower; the room had its own elevator and was operated by Henry, who, surely must have been a veteran of the Spanish War. I'm sure he had a last name but I never asked. For me, working there was akin to putting a rabbit to guard the cabbage patch. The second reason was social, I met any number of co-eds there, and the third, since we had classes on Saturdays in those days, and the English Department demanded an essay a week during the Freshman year, my roommates Fred Kyle (Sherman), the late T. O. Wilson (Rosenberg) and John Dalrymple (Little Rock) would fold their books and we'd walk to Memorial Stadium after closing time, one o'clock. All Southwest Conference games started in the blistering heat at two P.M. Student seating was excellent, on the sunny side, of course, but our seats went from one 30-yard line to the other. We could sit anywhere, up or down, and we all owned the blanket tax, a multipurpose card which served as an I.D. at the library and as entry to all, that's *all,* athletic events.

These, the four of us attended religiously; well, as religiously as T. O. and I attended St. Austen; Kyle, a fine Scottish name, was a Presbyterian, and Dalrymple, from Arkansas, a Baptist; no surprise there.

A disappointment, the *F* I received in Geology. This is what happened: The professor, a man named Stafford who affected a British intonation, said, during the first day of classes, that no hourly tests were to be missed, that no excuses would be accepted and if one missed an hourly, this would result in a failing grade.

Well, my father died at two in the morning on the day of the exam. My oldest brother, Roy Lee, called me at Cliff Courts. There were no phones in the hutments; one went outside to a public telephone which some students abused by inserting a coin in the nickel slot and, using a screwdriver, would spin the coin down the chute to make the Southwestern Bell ring. The tool was kept by a junior student called Willie the Lion, not to be confused with the great stride pianist since there were no Black Texans enrolled at the time. While I'd been away in the Army, Heman Marion Sweatt had fought to be enrolled and had done so through the courts. Now there's a building on campus named for him; the word "irony" comes to mind.

Friends from home had arranged for a pilot and his Piper Cub to pick me up at what passed for Austin's airport at the time. We buried my father, and I rode the bus back to Austin. I believed Stafford's dictum about failure if one missed the exam, and I didn't go to his office. Hence, the F. I signed up for Geology again and, with help of a friendly co-ed, whom I helped with her advanced Spanish course, I earned a B both semesters. That was the only F. I was on the G.I. Bill (confession time). I enjoyed seeing my name on the Dean's List and imagined my mother's smiling face when she received the grades sent by the university, which is the way it was done in those days.

The Co-op was where the Co-op is, without its many additions and subtractions; one could listen to music in the basement in any of the three booths so provided. The Co-op also carried more books at the time when slide rules, the contemporary computers, were put to good use.

I represented my college in Student Government one year (we were called Aldermen in those days) and there existed deep social and political divides in the student body between MICA and WICA (Men's Independent College Association and the Women I.C.A.) and The Clique, as the social organizations were called and so referred to in *The Daily Texan* under Ronnie Dugger and later, Willie Morris.

I was also a member of the Tejas Club and later became a Pike, a card-carrying member of the Pi Kappa Alpha fraternity; the use of *frat* was frowned upon in those days and no fraternity man used it; at least not in public. My good friend and fellow Tejas man, Lynn Beason (who later, after service in the Philippines as a marine lieutenant, attended law school and joined the old Coke and Coke firm in Dallas) became a Deke while retaining his Tejas membership. I remember talking about these relationships with Jack Holland, Dean of Men (now called something else, I believe), and he said he saw no problem if Beason and I didn't, and that was it. The other dean, Arno Nowotny served, I believe, as Dean of Student Life, whatever that meant. A native of New Braunfels, if I'm not mistaken. Typical of the times of *loco parentis*.

I loved my classes except those I took in the College of Education; I did my practice teaching at the old Austin High on 12th Street, and I earned a B as I did in all my classes where an A was the usual order of the day, whether one slept during class or not. I wanted to teach and my high GPA suffered on account of the Bs. Unlike today, an A was worth three points, a B two and so on. A D was a passing grade but carried no points.

Talk about a lack of grade inflation in those times.

Biology was something else; we worked in two-person teams and began with a fetal pig; my partner, first name Barry, wanted to be a naval aviator but he wasn't about to touch a dead fetus. After this came a sheep's heart, a cow's eye and we would wind up with an earthworm. I found this fascinating while Barry, hands in pockets, entertained me with jokes and stories. We passed with flying colors and took our lectures and lab work at the old Biology Building now called Painter Hall and named for Theophilus Schickel Painter, the man who, as president, signed René's diploma; mine was signed by Logan Wilson, a recent acquisition from Chapel Hill.

My brother wore his ring proudly but neglected to pick up his diploma. I solved this by walking across from the Reading Room into the Registrar's Office, said hello to one of the students who worked there who then led me to a sizable wire cage full of unclaimed diplomas stuffed in those round, hardcover mailing containers. I mailed it to René,who placed it next to his USS *Mississippi* shipmates' group photograph.

My diploma? Someone broke into my car at the Brownsville High School parking lot and took it. I imagine the thief saw no value in it and threw it away. I discovered it in a muddy pond in front of the football stadium. Ruined, of course, and that was it.

Movie houses. Four, as I remember: the Texas, in front of the Texas Union, and the Varsity, both on Guadalupe. The Texas exhibited many foreign films to packed houses; one had to read the subtitles and I suppose this may be too much for some students who have better things to do than to sit through English, French and Italian movies. The Texas also showed operas on film; I remember *Rigoletto, The Marriage of Figaro* and *Madama Butterfly*. The Varsity stuck to Hollywood films.

Faculty. I, along with my fellow undergraduates, had no idea of professorial rankings: teaching assistants, assistant professors and so on. On the first day of classes, and this was common, someone would ask if we were to address the instructor as Dr. or Mr. (few women in UT's faculty then.) The proper title must've been a touchy subject. The following occurred in American History, a sophomore class and a legislative requirement. The class included two students who enrolled with René in '46. Not to brag, but I earned a 100 in the 100 identification questions; the two, each, made a 12. One, and I forget which, but remember exactly what he said, asked me, "Do you think they'll curve the grades?"

The legislative requirement also held for the sophomore government class. One registered at Gregory Gym where, at the entrance, stood boxes filled with small pieces of paper asking if we were or had been, at one time or another, a member of subversive organizations. The Black Dragon Society is one I remember well. One was supposed to sign the chits. Ha! The boxes either remained filled or were emptied on the steps of that fine old building. Gregory also served as the site for global examinations as did Hogg Auditorium, where we sat in alternate seats and in alternate rows; the old honor system. In Hogg, the cement floors served as pencil sharpeners. One held up one's stub, the proctors gave the okay, and thus the pencils were sharpened. Rumors regarding wholesale cheating were common. A favorite myth centered on Freddy Phi Gam, a St. Bernard, said to wander casually into a classroom and 1) carry the answers in his collar, or 2) walk out and take the answers home when someone complained of Freddy's presence. Interesting if true, but I thought that anyone who believed that whopper must've fallen off a turnip truck.

Aside from basketball, Gregory was also used for dances, plays and invited speakers. Hogg, too, but for smaller crowds where one enjoyed the San Antonio Symphony and a riot of a comedy show written and acted by students, *Time Staggers On.* One of the actresses was a Corpus Christi native who played the role of Lungs Bedlow and who much later played Barney Miller's wife in the popular TV sitcom. Varsity Carnival, alas, has disappeared. It was held in the intramural fields, which also housed sixteen high-fenced tennis courts and next to them, three 80-yard long football fields, which also served as soccer fields or three softball diamonds.

Fame being a fleeting thing, I doubt the majority of Texans remember Jane Holcomb who, I was told, was a Miss Texas. Her seat, next to mine in Geology usually went unfilled (the class numbered some 300) but someone would sit in her place, and she would then be marked present. The teaching assistants took roll by looking at their seating arrangement charts and at the row number; later, the Geology building housed the Hogg Foundation for Medical Health. By the way, Miss Ima's name is pronounced Eema. And there was no Ura.

Yes, it was a small campus, and the women's swimming pool, named for professor Anna Hiss, stood behind the new Experimental Science building. The men's Olympic-sized pool was in Gregory. In those days, one took a foot bath before diving in, tight-fitting swimming caps were de riguer, but swimming trunks were not allowed. And how's that for the uptight '50s?

THE GULF OIL-CAN SANTA CLAUS
(1983)

B y the time the Japanese Imperial Forces were deep into the
mopping-up operations in the Bataan Peninsula, preparations
for the siege and fall of Corregidor were also under way. One of
the defenders was Clemente García, a twenty-three-year-old
youngster from Mercedes, Texas, down in the Valley.

He was born not in Mercedes but in northern Mexico; his
mother, two brothers and a sister had crossed the Río Grande at
Río Rico, Tamaulipas, Mexico, and settled in Mercedes some two
or three years after the death of Don Clemente senior, a victim of
the Spanish influenza epidemic in the twenties.

Don Clemente had been a veteran of the Mexican Revolution:
upon his death, as he was an enlisted careerman, his widow began
to receive a smallish pension from the Mexican government.

Mrs. García's decision to cross the Río Grande was an economic one and thus no different from that made by hundreds of
thousands of European and other immigrants who settled in the
United States. The choice of Mercedes was no accident, however:

many newly arrived Mexican nationals made it a type of halfway house before they spread out all over Texas, the Midwestern United States and beyond.

Of the many Garcías, these settled in Mercedes. Aurora, an only daughter, did needlepoint and constructed some remarkably intricate paper designs used as cemetery decorations. Two of the youngsters, Arturo and Medardo, were apprenticed off to neighborhood *panaderías*—bakeries. Clemente, clearly the brightest, according to the family, enrolled at the all-Texas-Mexican neighborhood school, North Ward Elementary.

He logged in the mandatory six years there and, at age 16, had learned to read and write enough English to hire on as a sackboy for a local grocery store. Later on he became the delivery man as well as the driver.

On his 21st birthday, he came to our home and knocked on the east porch door. I was the only one home at the time and invited him in. He thanked me but said he was in the middle of a delivery; he had stopped, he said, to ask my father's advice on some matter, but that he'd call again.

Our people came to the Valley, as had his, with the Escandón expedition and colonists of 1749. Our family happened to live on the northern bank of the Río Grande when it became part of the American Union; his ancestors had lived on the southern bank, and thus, with the proclamation of the Treaty of Guadalupe Hidalgo, they became Mexican nationals, and we, American citizens.

Since Clemente had no father, he called on mine for advice; this was in the late thirties, and there were still some strong remnants of the old-patriarchal system established in 1750. "It's a serious matter, don Manuel," he said to my father.

This was the obligatory phrase, and it could encompass almost anything, from a request for my father, as a sponsor, to ask for a girl's hand in marriage to putting in a good word—*dar una recomendación,* for whatever was needed. In short, almost anything, but certainly something of importance to the petitioner.

The Great Depression was still hanging on in the Valley and elsewhere, and steady jobs were hard to come by. In Clemente's case, though, it was something different: during one of his deliveries in the Anglo Texan side of town, he had met a man named Claude Rodgers. According to Clemente, Rodgers was going to own and operate a Gulf Oil gas station in the Texas-Mexican part of town. And Rodgers had asked Clemente if he wanted to work there, full-time. Clemente had not known what to say to this, but Rodgers solved that when he said, "Think it over. Come by in a week or so."

My father listened to Clemente, nodded and then pointed to a chair. Clemente sat down, and one of my sisters brought him a tall glass of limeade. I was about to leave them, but my father said I could stay, and I did so.

The upshot was that he took the job; the gas station was directly across the street from our house, and I would see him every day on my way to and from North Ward Elementary.

In November 1940, a week before Thanksgiving, as I was crossing North Texas Avenue on my way home, I heard a series of shrill whistles: it was Clemente. "*Acá,*" he said. "Over here," he grinned and yelled out, "*Ándale.* Come on, hurry it up." He was standing under the car wash and surrounded by Gulf Oil cans.

"What's up?" I asked.

"Look." And he pointed.

"At what? The oil cans?"

"Yeah, I've been saving them."

"Can you sell 'em, like milk bottles?"

He laughed then and said, "No. I'm going to weld them, all of them. I'm going to weld them and make us a Santa Claus for Christmas."

"Really? Out of cans?"

"Yeah, you just wait."

"Can I help?"

"You better, it's my Christmas present for you."

"For me?"

"Sure. We'll begin by rinsing them and drying them out. What's your dad going to give you?"

"A pair of khaki pants. And a leather belt, from Matamoros."

"And this'll be your third Christmas present; everybody's entitled to three, you know. Like *los magos,* the Magi."

Thanksgiving came and went, and every afternoon, after running errands and doing the daily chores, I'd run over to Rodgers' Gulf, rinse some more cans and watch Clemente weld them for the Santa Claus.

"We're going to put it up there, on top of the car wash. I'll get some good, strong wire and nothing'll blow it down; not even the Gulf wind."

Clemente finished it a week before Christmas, and then in January, on the Day of the Magi, he received a notice from the local Selective Service Board.

He took and passed his physical in San Antonio in March 1941, and he was on his way to the Philippines by October of the same year. What letters he wrote to his mother were brought to my father to read. My father also translated the fateful telegram sent by the War Department in the summer of '42.

The Santa Claus stayed on top of the car wash for some 10 years after World War II. Rusted out, finally, but I remembered it was big and red and white and held there by big, black boots. Perfect.

In the way of the world of the living, I forgot about it, and I had almost forgotten Clemente García, "La Norteñita." It was an affectionate name, and feminine; but he was called that, in the singular, in honor of his favorite song, "Las Norteñitas," "Those Oh-so-sweet Northern Girls."

Then, one December day, I went down to Mercedes on some now-forgotten family business. Urban renewal had taken care of Rodgers' Station and the house in which I was born. In its place, there was a parking lot, but across the street, Rodgers' station had been replaced by a tire store; it was owned by a man named Leopoldo Martínez.

As I crossed the street to see Martínez, I thought I saw the Gulf Oil-can Santa Claus. I walked on, and I was sure I had seen it again. Somewhere.

I ran inside the store and then almost knocked down a clerk taking inventory.

"Oh, it's you, Doctor. How are you?"

I stopped and looked at him for some sign of recognition but found none.

"I'm sorry," I said. "Who's your father?"

"Leocadio Gavira, the truck driver; he knows you."

I nodded and apologized again. He couldn't help noticing my searching for something and asked, "Can I help you?"

I didn't know what to say, where to begin. Images of the thirties, forties and fifties flicked on and off again as in a slide show until I finally said, "No . . . thanks; I thought I had seen something . . . it's nothing." He nodded, and as I turned to go, the image flashed on again, as a reflection somewhere.

Why, it was nothing more than a blown-up Michelin Man waving and smiling at me. Someone had painted him up as Santa Claus.

The Gavira youngster looked at it and said: "Oh, that. It's a new tire line. You know, some of the older people come in and stare at it for the longest time. You know why they do that?"

I nodded slightly and on an impulse asked, "Did you ever know or hear of the Widow García on Hidalgo and First?"

"Sure, she must be close to ninety, ninety-five, a hundred, maybe. She's still alive, you know; lives with a daughter, I think."

And with her silent memories, I added silently.

"Thanks . . . what's your name"

"John, sir."

"John! Well, thanks, again."

"Yes, sir." And he went back to his inventory.

The Michelin Tire Man. It looked grotesque, somehow, but —and again somehow—it looked like my third Christmas present, my Gulf Oil-can Santa Claus, the one I got before the war.

A FEW NOTES ON TRANSLATION
(2008)

When I was at the age with a single digit, and what follows is family lore, I had learned to read Spanish at age five. My mother, who had taught for a while, had taught me to read English at home by age four. I come from a family of readers—my parents read to each other and I, as the youngest, took my oldest brothers and sister as models (being dirt poor, we didn't have siblings in those days). I was also a sickly child and this afforded me much time to devote to reading.

In those days, San Antonio published *La Prensa* with a wide readership of Texas Mexicans as well as Mexican nationals who lived in the Valley as a result of the twists and turns of the Mexican Revolution of 1910 which, seemingly, lasted forever. And so, the first formal schooling I received was at a local Mexican school, which we called "la escuelita" and taught, in the main, by Mexican nationals. The paper was sent by rail throughout the state. Added to this, *The Brownsville Herald* also published the Spanish edition on a daily basis. *El Heraldo de Brownsville*. A relative of mine, as we say, *un pariente*, Américo Paredes, worked on both editions; he also contributed poetry, which was published in *La Prensa*'s *Los lunes literarios*, the Monday Literary Supplement. And, it was in this literary supplement that I first read Honoré Balzac and Guy de Maupassant. Strange names, I took them for Spanish Basques.

It wasn't until years later, high school, the military, the university, that I learned who they were and discovered I'd been reading translations all along. This was a surprise since our high school teachers, and we had two in that small high school, were rigorous in regard to usage, clarity, punctuation, grammar and what makes the language work. They also encouraged creativity when one reached the junior year in a compilation of student writing titled *Creative Bits*. For all this, as encouraging as it was, there was no mention of world literature and thus no mention of available translations.

This preamble, and I hope it hasn't been too much of a trial, was necessary for the following: as a member of the English Department at Austin, one of the points I make to my literature classes concerns their reading of world literature for enjoyment and for the pleasure of reading of other cultures and countries. For instance, in Plan II, the University's designation of the Honors Classes in the College of Liberal Arts, I teach Homer and some of the Greek dramatists, and it is possible for me to do so because of the fine translations available. Since in the state of Texas, and I suspect in most of the remaining forty-nine, Latin instruction exists in few of the 254 counties in this state. The same goes for the Catholic schools where the majority of teachers now are lay personnel who were deprived of studying Latin, with few exceptions. It's a sad and widespread loss but not a total loss if one talks to dedicated public school English teachers who teach some of the classics in English. So, all is not lost, but it is difficult in an age where, according to some of my students, commas should be placed where they *think* they should go.

That, of course, was a digression, but I confess I remain impenitent when it comes to digressions. Not all translations are valuable, we know that, and Cervantes, for one, is a case in point. As many of us here know, the English have remained keen in regard to Peninsular literature; I have read and seen so through the years that the *Times Literary Supplement* carries finely wrought articles on Spanish literature. I did a brief and broad rather than extensive and intensive study of translations of Don Quijote, beginning with Thomas Shelton's translation of the first volume six years after its appearance in Spain, and then, when the second was published posthumously, Shelton was there again with his translation six years hence. There was a bit of a surprise when I came across Toby Smollet's translation; in many instances, he did what master painters did, he had auxiliary help with some of the passages to the detriment of Cervantes' work. My first brush with the English *Don Quixote* came from reading Putnam; I found it an enlightenment and kept it for years only to pass it on to a nephew who couldn't and didn't read Spanish. Years later, I then read Burton Raffel's fine work and championed it for years by recommending it to men and women who had heard about but not read Cervantes' work. Raffel's work is first rate, there's no question. But it was a friend, a good friend, Jim Parr out in California, who recommended Edith Grossman's work. There may be other translations, for if translators love anything, it's a challenge. But I must confess that Edith Grossman's work is, as we say in Spanish, "un encanto." It works; this is not to disparage Raffel or my old Putnam, it's that she has captured that "duende" that Federico García Lorca wrote about. No, I don't sit at home and read a page by Raffel and then the same page by Grossman; that's an insult to both. And, what I am offering is an opinion, not an established fact. But the point is, that without translators we would be poorer; it takes fine writing to survive, say, as nineteenth-century Russian literature survived despite, what my friends at Illinois claimed, were poor, troubling, French translations. On the other hand, the English translations may have just saved that Golden Age of Russian Literature.

Now I don't know and it hasn't been my pleasure to meet, and thus to thank Leila Vennevitz for making me fall in love with Heinrich Böll's work. I didn't meet him either, although I had the chance with the good offices of a friend of his; I did, though, spend an afternoon with René, one of his sons, and with Marie who was still bright and lively until time, that implacable enemy of us all, took first, her mind, then her body. And no, I never mentioned his name or his work. We talked about Ireland, where they had a home and where they lived for a while. I don't believe she's translated anyone's work, but her English, with lovely American-Irish-English intonations made for a lovely afternoon in Marten. For those among us who read and appreciate Böll, the town cemetery is close to their home; as a champion of the Roma people, they've festooned his gravesite with curious gifts, year after year. In passing, there are several nuns buried in that small cemetery as well as the remains of young American aviators downed not far from the village.

Another digression, I'm afraid. What follows, briefly, is my work as a self-translator. I didn't dare translate my work and let ten years go by before I did so and then, another ten before I attempted the second. I've taken some heat, but it's laughable since those who complained of my own and of my work on Tomás Rivera's work came from Texas and California Mexicans, who, in the main, are, for the most part, not only monolingual but also monocultural. For all us here know it isn't enough, not by a long chalk, that knowledge of the language is the only arrow in a translator's quiver. Not at all; history is also involved, and I'm saying nothing new to us here who are professional translators, but without historical and cultural knowledge and familiarity, the odds of a sensitive rendition of the target language are long; poor translations are in long supply.

Knowledge of a people's culture, to use a mathematical term, it not only important, it is also essential. We know how we react to some literal translations; accurate, perhaps, but instructive as to the place and time, no, not always on target, I believe. Here, knowledge of the culture enters into the fray and challenge: idiomatic expressions often times are an aid to the work at hand, because they are not stilted, but there has to be a happy medium somewhere, and the bridges we depend on are the translators. The chief reason for this, from where I sit, is that creativity plays, as all of us who engage in translation know, not only a large part, but also a challenge when one chooses a word or a phrase only to erase it, to replace it and then, often enough, to return to the original phrase. That, colleagues, is creativity.

And that is the chief reason I accepted Steve Kelman's kind invitation; I once attended, by invitation, an American Translators Association conference at UT Dallas where I was happy to meet, for the first time, men and women, who had brought me a happy understanding of what it meant to work with two languages at the same time. I remain grateful to UT Dallas for the opportunity and, having lived this long, I'm now in debt to UTSA's Steve Kelman and to you who've been patient, so far, with a self-translator. Thank you.

CHICANO LITERATURE: AN AMERICAN
LITERATURE WITH A DIFFERENCE
(1981)

C ontemporary Chicano literature may be subdivided into several categories: that one written in English, the one written in
Spanish and, in some cases, the one employing both languages.
Further subdivisions could be the urban versus the rural setting or
that which presents the cultural nationalistic point of view, and so
forth.

I think it is clear that few existing U.S. literatures present much
of a language choice. American Literature, on the other hand, does
present language choices; by American literature, then, I mean, as
Jose Martí did, the Americas, meaning the whole of the Western
Hemisphere.

Much of the early work of Chicano literature, as well as the contemporary one of twenty years back, was utilitarian, particularly the
poetry and, in some cases, the shorter prose. By utilitarian I choose
to mean that which was at once didactic to those in the culture
—for its reaffirmative or reassuring stance—and to those outside
the culture as a means of explication as to who these Spanish-

speaking or bilingual/bicultural Americans were about. It is now obvious that conflicting and often contradictory messages were being sent out to both cultures.

One example of conflicting reports should suffice for now and should also open up certain areas of discussion: in the early days, invariably, almost every writer claimed to be bearer of the Chicano word.

I'll now touch briefly on the academy and the dissemination of the literature. U.S. Mexicans, to use that as a conventional term, were publishing and writing many years prior to the Civil Rights movements of the sixties. These same sixties also saw the rise of other ethnopoetic literatures: the Asian-American, the Native-American and an increased awareness and productivity of the established Black-American Literature. The sixties also witnessed the birth of Quinto Sol Publications, a publishing house started by a group of junior professors and students at the University of California at Berkeley. The advent of Quinto Sol in an academic center proved to be the germination of later university-based publishers, and thus one saw the rise of the *Revista Chicano Riqueña,* first at Indiana University and now at the University of Houston; the Bilingual Review Press at York College first and later on at Eastern Michigan University, and now at SUNY-Binghamton; *Maize* at the University of California at San Diego and other publication endeavors as well. Some of the rewards of this early academic setting, by the way, have been the recent publications on Chicano literature by the University of Texas Press, an extensive bibliography published by the Chicano Center at U.C. Berkeley, and now a recently published history of the literature in the Twayne series. Without going into some of the obvious merits and demerits of the works themselves, this American literature can be judged to be not only surviving here and there, but thriving as well because of increased publications and academic support.

Another of its distinguishing characteristics, or differences, at this stage, is the international recognition it has received in the span of a few years. Improved communications between peoples may be one factor of its recognizability; its quality may be another. In the academy, one of the differences is that this literature is read in departments of English, Spanish, American Studies, and in the other humanities and social sciences. During the academic revolution of the sixties when stultified curricula underwent radical changes, Chicano literature happened to arrive at the precise historical moment for inclusion in the various curricula.

Given the usual in-fighting that we've all experienced in our various disciplines, the inclusion of Chicano literature was not an easy process, as one can imagine, and it shouldn't have been easy. It was right that it be questioned and tested, that it be examined and held under some very bright lights, and it couldn't and shouldn't have been done in any other way, if it were to survive.

This said, I'll now follow with a necessary digression: One need not go more than thirty years in this country, 1953, say, to prove my following point: I invite everyone to look to your own MLA bibliographies for the number of bibliographical entries for Hispanic-American Literature for those times. It was not until 1957 when the National Defense Education Act was proposed and later enacted that Hispanic-American Literature came into its own in this country. Mexicanists and other Hispanic Americanists enjoyed, if that's the word, a minority status in the old Romance Language departments, until they claimed the larger number of graduate students as time went on in the 60's and 70's—yesterday, as it were. It is safe to say that those active 1980's Hispanic-American scholars are, for the most part, post 1956-60 Ph.D.s.

So much, then, for tradition in the curricula.

And here's another contradiction: Chicano literature, which at times passed itself off as a people's literature, was really a child, is actually a child of us, the academicians who make up one of the last of the privileged classes in our native land. (I say privileged because we are deferred due to our expertise in some instances and because we have the time for reflection; as is often the case, many of us also have time for academic mischief, but that's another story.)

I'll now touch briefly on the readership and on the birth of this contemporary American literature. I'll begin with the second. Since, for the most part, the university was its pediatric ward, a certain stability for the continuance of its reading was insured, much like—and this will hit close to home—much like the continuance of other literatures is insured when taught at the academy. I'll explain by asking two questions: How many volumes of Chaucer and Mío Cid, of Shakespeare and Cervantes, of Pérez Galdós and Hardy would be read in the fifty states semester after semester, quarter after quarter, were it not for all of us who attempt to teach them to our undergraduate students? We contribute to some of their understanding, of course, but we also subsidize these fine authors. How many volumes would be published to be bought and read by the general public? The same can be asked of Chicano literature, but the difference is the following: countless conversations with students and colleagues at numerous conferences reveal that Chicano students do not, as a rule, sell their literature books back to the bookstore; instead, they take them home to their parents and relatives. And thus it is they who propagate the literature. I have no idea how long the practice will continue, but if it goes on, it points to a further cementing of the literature and its academic base. Now, in the 1980s, there are increasing instances of second- and third-generation U.S. Mexican students at the universities; these students avail themselves of the various Chicano offerings and they enroll in these classes as a matter of course; their parents did not because they could not, but now they too enjoy the books.

The wide range of usage and readership may not increase sales dramatically, but when Rivera's . . . *and the earth did not part* or my *Klail City Death Trip Series,* for two examples, are used in courses in Psychology, Social Work, History, Sociology, Education and in the various literature courses mentioned, this, among other things, means that this fiction has as wide an application as it possibly can in terms of versatility and utility. In some ways, then, it is a people's literature.

There are, then, historical reasons for this phenomenon; for now, one need not go farther back than the sixties and the already mentioned civil rights movements. It happens, however, that the literature had existed before that time. Much of it was ready to come out as a result of encouragement, in some cases, but also because it was its time to come out then. And come out it did. Since the base was an academic one, book titles were needed and the majority population publishing houses attempted to meet the sudden demand. One of the consequences of this demand in this newly discovered market was the publication and dissemination of some mediocre material; but, mediocre or not, a void needed to be filled and soon there was a union of convenience. As you can certainly imagine, much of this welter fell by the wayside; not all of it, no, and not immediately either, but time is a great leveller, and a lot of that early literature sank without a trace, and no great loss, I say.

But time also brings new developments, and in time, other writers began to write and to publish in this country and abroad. The difference this time was that this American literature was being read in Spanish here and in Spanish-speaking America and, as in any other literature, in translation in various European countries.

It's strange, and perhaps it is far more accurate to say different than strange, when one considers the exportation of a U.S. literature in a language other than English, and this is what happened to this literature.

Time—again and as always—will be the ultimate judge. And time will also be the witness when one language eventually overwhelms the other in Chicano literature. With increased urbanization and changes in the culture, English may win out as the dominant language, but there is no guarantee that I'll be proven correct in this regard. The Spanish language, as any other language, may undergo certain linguistic changes, and thus both languages may continue side by side; one never knows.

In closing, I'll say that when Álvar Núñez made his trip from Florida to Texas in the sixteenth century, he was somehow laying the foundation of a future American literature written in Spanish, north of the Rio Grande. As the saying goes, "uno nunca sabe para quién trabaja" and this literature written by U.S. Mexicans is a constant reminder of a Spanish presence here, in what most of us, I dare say, can legally call our native land. Chicano literature is a U.S. literature, but it is also a literature of our Americas, as Martí so clearly saw and labelled the New World.

REDEFINING AMERICAN LITERATURE
(1991)

I n the fall of 1896, William Lyon Phelps was an assistant professor at Harvard, and he introduced the concept of an American
literature in the United States for the very first time. He chose Poe
and Hawthorne, Melville, Whitman and Dickinson. In the ensuing
semester he was told to stop teaching, and I'm quoting, that "so-
called American literature." He was threatened with dismissal.
Phelps went on, of course, as we already know, to agitate for the
inclusion of American literature in American colleges and universities. That "so-called literature" phrase may sound familiar when
one thinks of Américo Paredes, for one, who established the Center for Mexican-American Studies at the University of Texas,
Austin, and of the men and women at other institutions who established Chicano Studies programs in the late sixties.

Now, as for Phelps, I doubt very much if it entered his head to
include, say, African-American literature or to wonder if there
were any other American literatures except his New England variety. However, his stance is understandable. American literature,

though, even the New England variety, was by no means widely accepted in the United States, or rather in university curricula, despite the later presence of Crane, Twain, Dean Howells, Dreiser and so on. I should like to add two additional facts. The first is that the first Ph.D. in American literature is a twentieth-century phenomenon. The second is that it wasn't until after World War II that a terminal degree in that literature was added to the curriculum in America's heartland, Kansas and Missouri.

American literature professors of the time faced the same problems, headaches and opposition to its offerings as did the professors of Hispanic-American literature in the Romance language departments in this country for the first fifty years of this century. It wasn't until after 1957 that Hispanic Americanists began to carve out their own territory in Romance language departments. The National Defense Education Act was largely responsible for the widening of Hispanic-American literature. The newness of Hispanic-American literature offerings in departments of Spanish and Portuguese may be appreciated when one learns that Luis Leal, one of the contributors to this volume, produced over fifty Ph.D. theses while at the University of Illinois (he's still very much alive and kicking at the University of California, Santa Barbara) and that the first thesis on Carlos Fuentes was not published until the sixties under his guidance.

The offerings in the Hispanic-American literature were augmented by waves of Central and South American literary scholars who migrated to the United States and taught in U.S. universities. The opposition by Peninsularists is a well-known recorded and unalterable fact. Their opposition does not differ much from that of the British literature specialists vis-a-vis Americanists. I don't pretend to know the entire history in this regard, but in the mid-fifties, when I was an undergraduate student at the University of Texas, the Romance language department offered two survey courses: a third-year junior course and a fourth-year senior and graduate course, both in Peninsular literature. The Hispanic-American literature courses were the following: the novel, including *Los de abajo* (The Underdogs), *La vorágine* (The Vortex), *Don Segundo Sombra* and *Doña Barbara;* two courses in the short story, both taught by Ms. Nina Weisinger, an adjunct professor who'd been an adjunct for forty years; and a senior graduate course, Mexican Literature, taught by Dorothy Schons. I also took *El Periquillo Sarniento* (The Itching Parrot) as a seminar, but that was the extent of the offerings of Hispanic-American literature in that Romance language department of so many years ago.

I'm offering this bit of archaeology to remind us that entering into the curriculum has never been easy for anyone. With the admission of a few courses in American literature at a few U.S. universities, one may be quite right in inferring that African-American literature was not offered at the time. Personally, I also doubt if anyone thought of it as an offering. I've not studied some of the offerings at Howard or Bishop College or at some of the other black institutions, but I think it would be instructive for all of us to do so, to see what it was that they were offering at the time.

Certain historical processes were going on in this country in the decade of the sixties. While the processes addressed the increase of enrollment of Americans of Mexican descent in U.S. colleges and universities, an adjunct to this was a demand for the hiring of Chicano professors and the teaching of college courses with reference and with relevance to our historical presence in our native land, the United States. The opposition to these demands was not long in coming; for a decade or so, well into the seventies, the demands were met at times, forgotten and fought, resisted, addressed repeatedly, admitted, rejected and so on. None of this is over, yet. But the modest increase of students was, and is, a visible piece of evidence. Not so is the increase of professors, but time may take care of this.

As for the course offerings, these are placed mostly in the college of liberal arts and within the colleges in departments, in centers and in programs. The opposition to the inclusion of Mexican American literature was understandable, if one accepts the opposition on academic grounds. That is, is there such an American literature? Who are its contributors? Is there a body of criticism? And so on. The answer to the last question was "no"—there was no body of criticism. But the answer was "yes" to the first two questions —the literature existed and exists, and people were contributing and had contributed to it. The next question: "Is it any good?" was also brought up. Well, none of us knew the answer to that, nor did William Lyon Phelps back in 1896. He had, of course, touched on William Bradford and Edward Taylor and Jonathan Edwards, William Cullen Bryant and James Fenimore Cooper. But he had focused on Poe, Hawthorne, Melville, Whitman and Dickinson.

Now, as to its worth and the widening of this American literature, this lies with time, and that's the only answer that anyone can actually say and admit because time is the great leveler, and it usually decides what will live and what will not. It so happens, however, that universities are repositories of learning and that our time in the academy is different front the time of those outside the university. It takes us a longer time to admit or to reject ideas or theories. We're not a shopping mall with bright lights and colors and soft music to persuade us toward one item or another. We're deliberate, and we debate, and we study, we argue, and we assess. Time is on our side, and long after the popular mind has dismissed or has forgotten that which is transitory, the academy investigates and meets, and it tables or acts upon it. We're often accused of talking something to death, and we may be found guilty of that, too. But we also have higher responsibilities, we are a university. We're not a supermarket where the customer is always right. The inclusion of any course or program brings curiosity and questions. It may also bring blind opposition. But then our universities are populated by all manner of colleagues who also possess all manner of ideas and opinions. Some, of course, are also paranoic, but we live with them, too.

The proposal to adopt African-American literature and literature of the Native American and the Asian-American and so on came in the sixties. The opposition on academic grounds was wanting, but the opposition on the basis of racism was something else. There was some of both; there was also some paranoia on both sides. But worse than paranoia, there was arrant racial prejudice and, as always in life, there was irony. Opposition came also from some Americanists who were teaching American literature, American literature in its narrowest sense, of course. For if one thinks that New England literature looked kindly upon Southern White literature, one would be mistaken, and let me remind us that it is not until the fifties that systematic studies in American literature began to appear in public institutions. Regarding Southern literature, at the time of Faulkner's winning of the Nobel Prize almost all of his books were out of print. The year was 1949, and American literature became a growing concern in the fifties.

The greater demand for American literature, the New England and the Southern variety, coincided with the increased enrollment in U.S. institutions after 1957. The enrollment, too, was selective, but I'm going to let that pass for a more important consideration: academic amnesia. Those who inherited ready-made degree programs in American literature opposed the widening of American literature. Since this is a young field, we have every right to suspect that many of these colleagues had not yet won their own spurs and here they were unwilling to read, let alone teach, Richard Wright, Langston Hughes, the younger Ralph Ellison, James Baldwin, Tomás Rivera, Lucy Topahanso, Denise Chavez, Jenny Chin, Wendy Rose and so on. One of the chief reasons was that American literature was still insecure as to its own place and standing in the curriculum, and because of this, it covered its own flanks and retrenched. While William Lyon Phelps had ample reason for his ignorance and for his narrow selection, our contemporary colleagues did not. They chose instead to retrench, to reject out of hand and, mistakenly, they went on to the other side of our other colleagues in British literature.

But let us see what happened. In 1968 the Modern Language Association was headed by Henry Nash Smith; that's a brief twenty-three years ago. In the late seventies Smith, along with Bill Schaefer, began to widen MLA representation and representative curriculum. Many of us know that Henry Nash Smith died not too long ago and those of us who knew him mourn his passing. Because it was he who, as a very strong force in the MLA, oversaw the changes in this country's curriculum in higher education. It would be an exaggeration to claim that Smith caused the changes, and he would not have made the claim, anyway; but as a leader, he recognized that the changes had to be made, and he facilitated those changes which paved the way for wider participation by women in the profession and the likewise important participation by other members of the MLA, who heretofore had not been included in any participatory capacity. Those other members of MLA included us—the Mexicans, that is Americans of Mexican descent—as well as native African Americans, Native Americans, Asian Americans, all members of the MLA.

Along with this decision came the inclusion of other American literatures which had been ignored and fought and derided and insulted. But time brought changes. Because in time younger and not so young Americanists widened American literature. I've heard it said, quite mistakenly, that it was the swing of the pendulum. I have to say that there's no such thing. I don't believe in cosmic changes. It isn't, and it wasn't, a pendulum. It was an effective breach which was widened to include the whole of the United States literature, irrespective of language.

Nevertheless, changes are constant, and it is the widening of the curriculum that has produced a vibrancy, once again, to American literature. The vibrancy has produced a breach in some of the old ideologies and in some of the old intramuralism and has served to introduce other voices.

I've no idea where it will end, but the ideas of 1967 regarding American literature are not those of 1991. This is the way it should be, since literature is meant to reflect values held and decisions taken by men and women and not by caricatures of them.

THE BAROQUE IN THE LIFE AND LITERATURE OF THE HISPANO-AMERICAN (1990)

As many of us know, the Baroque and the term, as well as its derivation and etymology, have long been in question and contention. The Italians claim it as theirs and so do the Portuguese, off and on; too, plausible explanations have been proposed and promoted for centuries by one camp or another. The German scholars came into the field of study when the Baroque was still thought of usually in the realm of architecture, and they continued their study when the Baroque also became a literary movement and thus a new field of study. The French enter into this as well, as one can suppose.

Needless to say, the Baroque was attacked when it first appeared on the scene. It was considered a danger—if not to public morals, although even this was advanced as an argument—to an established movement that (to the proponents of the Baroque) had stopped moving: the Classics. But what Classics? Well, there was classic architecture, art, music and, of course, classic literature.

Some of us here today also know something of the history of Romanticism, and this movement, too, was considered a danger when it appeared later on; it too was considered as a danger to public morals. What is Romanticism, anyway? was the question. What good does it do? Why do these people take this extreme view of life? Why do they behave the way they do?

What, after all, does it mean; what does it purport to do other than to revolutionize the existing order? The Baroque had faced similar questions earlier, of course. That term, existing order, gave the attackers away. Without saying it, they mean their existing order, that is, the Classic way. Never mind, of course, that nature, a favorite element of the Classics, had been shown to be revolutionary and evolutionary, ever moving and in constant motion away from what it had been, what it was and toward something new. Nature had and has a way of renovating itself, but the Classicists took the view that nature was constant and unchanging.

It was the Romantics pulling away from the so-called Classic mode that caused the consternation in much the same way that the Baroque had earlier upset the Classic artists and architects. To put it another way, the workers in the Baroque shook the Classic form and attempted to improve on it. This was quite a claim, for if something is classic, that is, perfect, then why paint the lily? Well, it had to do with change, not merely for change's sake, but for the necessity of changing something to keep it alive.

This sounds like a paradox, but let me explain: The Baroque, in architecture, did not seek to destroy the foundation, that is, that which props up the structure; it merely sought to change that part of the work which we could see; and, by doing so, it strived to show (us) the additions placed on the original works to make us see something new; the emperor was still there, but he had on new clothes which one could see rather than imagine. Although imagination also played an important role in the appreciation of the Baroque.

The reaction to change is one all of us know, and the traditionalists reacted accordingly. The traditionalists, the standard of all that was good and proper, that stood in the name of the natural order of things, saw the Baroque as a danger to their very philosophy, their way of life. These new people were considered usurpers, barbarians; they wanted to change a straight line—where there had always—that is, since the beginning of time—been a straight line. The walls, pilasters, nooks, crannies, apses, naves, why, nothing was safe from these usurpers of the established order. And, as always, the term order appeared as the rallying cry. Without order, they seemed to say, there is nothing.

But the so-called usurpers said, well, there is too much order, and too much of a good thing can't be that good for anyone. Let, then, the old order remain, but let's add something to it, let's bring some imagination, some daring, something, finally, that would be pleasing to both the eye and the mind. The eye could still see the orderly wall, but it could also see something else that could, in some ways, bring to it the pleasure that a straight, solid, classic wall could not.

There would be another change; the mind, too, could roam around aided by the eye which allowed it to imagine things that weren't there, things that could be imagined to be there. In brief, the Baroque promised something new, but it wasn't for the timid, for those who wanted something safe. Nor, did it promise reassurances of a return to, or the maintenance of, the past. It must have been somewhat frightening since the Baroque also did not promise continuity. I think you can see how this movement, for that's what it was, would prove unsettling for many people. A view of the original wall would change if one took, say, five steps to the left or five steps to the right. What the viewer saw was the same thing, but it wasn't the same thing; it was another paradox. Another breaking away from the familiar, a step toward the unknown, toward that which was exciting.

The same exciting changes took place in music and the other arts, as we know. No need to go into that here, but suffice it to say that we have all lived with the changes and thus profited from them. These were changes made not for novelty's sake; that role would be played by rococo art. One of the main differences between the two is well known: whereas the Baroque reacted against the Classic form and realized a life for itself, the rococo, which is still with us, is more of a survivor rather than a leader of a movement.

As regards coming head to head with an established order, I, as a U.S. Hispanic, and as an academic, see a marked congruence between the original established order of the literature programs in our universities and the once-startling introduction of Mexican-American literature into the curriculum. The congruence lies, chiefly, in the opposition the literature faced in the early seventies.

Some academicians with short memories forget that nineteenth- and twentieth-century American literature also faced opposition when it attempted to become part of our university curriculum. The opposition came from another quarter, those who taught British literature in our universities. The same can be said of the opposition faced by Latin Americanists when the language departments were dominated by Peninsular specialists. It took the infusion of money in the late 1950s to bring Latin American literature to a respectable representation in those departments. Water under the bridge? Perhaps.

Now, what you see before you this afternoon is a native son, born and reared in a region once inhabited by indigenous people along the lower Rio Grande Valley. That piece of land later became part of the Spanish Empire and still later, Mexico. In time it became part of the Republic of Texas followed in short order by becoming part of the Union, followed by the Confederacy and finally, the Union again.

These formal changes of governments took place within the lifetime of my paternal great, great-grandmother, Doña Mauricia Cano who was born in 1814 and who died in 1904.

These changes had less to them than met the eye, for a while there were formal governmental changes, the people maintained a social democracy common to rural communities. Too, the classic social rural forms were kept, and this helped to stabilize the place.

However, as in any borderland, there were constant shifts and changes, new additions, and these helped to bring vitality to the place. These changes, these leavenings, could be looked upon as the Baroque adding its spirit to the classic, rural, communal way of life.

By the time Doña Mauricia died in 1904, Texas had undergone Reconstruction and had been restored to the Union for thirty years. That bit of Texas facing the Gulf of Mexico was American soil and it presented well-known American institutions to the rest of the union: counties, public schools, regular elections and so on. But there was something else going on at the same time. The early English-speakers who lived and died there did so as bicultural American citizens. Many of them married and settled there; often-times they engaged in commerce on both sides of the river, and while remaining red-blooded Texans and American citizens, the Spanish language was not unknown to them. Spanish became not their second language but merely another means of expression among themselves and the original settlers.

The racial lines would blur at times and last names, such as Heath, Howell, Atkinson, Weaver, Kingsbury and Hull, would be merely that, last names and identifiers as to families but not as to racial stock necessarily. Thus the classic European names remained, but with Hispanic additions to them.

One could look at a plaque commemorating the dead of World War I, II, Korea and so on, read the names listed there, and see something different from what an outsider would see. The outsider would see names of French, English, German and Spanish deriva-tion as casualties. The outsider's eyes would also see a flat surface with names, while we would see differing configurations with extending and extensive bloodlines despite the varied European surnames. We would see lines crossing and crisscrossing across the years and across the wars that would cause the flat surfaces to show us another reality which I learned later on was refraction, one of the chief attributes of the Baroque.

I, of course, at a young age was innocent of such concepts. But it was the incessant phenomenon of refraction, of looking, say, at the same object in media of different densities, that caused one to see the illusion but to recognize its reality. This did not come all at once as in a blinding epiphany but rather in more gradual ways which, because of a great number of examples, seeped into the mind and was retained there much like a reservoir stores water; at this point, I should like to point out that water is a well-known and recurring symbol of the Baroque; in my case, it comes in double doses since being born in a farming community, water was not only important, it was essential. Too, one was always watchful either because of a drought or a flood. And then, there was the ever present Rio Grande, a jurisdictional barrier but not necessarily a cultural one.

Added to this, it was the examples through actions and reactions, that what one was taught and shown in school, and told there, was in refraction to what also one learned and heard there. To counter this, we, the Texas Mexicans, also had our own schools aside from the public ones. These schools were taught by Mexican exiles, men and women, who had crossed to the northern bank during one phase or another of the seemingly unending Mexican Revolution. Our parents paid fifty cents a month for our schooling, all in Spanish, of course our teachers were actors, that is, participants in a conflict to which our parents, American citizens, felt themselves obliged to take sides or to participate in.

This was pretty heady stuff for youngsters to take in, and yet this too became part of our lives, of this disparate, often discrete, manner of looking at life. And, since our special summer school was taught in Spanish, we would close the day by singing the Mexican national anthem. In September, when the regular school started, it was morning prayer and the Pledge of Allegiance. I very much doubt if either the prayer or the Pledge affected me emotionally either way. Both, however, impressed upon me a sense of a dual belonging, a duality which, years later I also learned was an important element of the Baroque. When the duality was fused, it became one more example proper to the Baroque.

But I think it was World War II that first established for me, and once and for all, that most Baroque of all elements, the brevity of life. If Harry Rouse, Hal Hoover and Gene Atteberry, in life, never spoke to Arnoldo Díaz or to Francisco and José González, it was death, that constant companion, that made these Mercedes, Texas natives, share the identical U.S. Government headstones.

That brevity of life, the skull behind the facial skin, awaited them all; and if it were true for them, why not for me, for everybody else, I asked myself. And meanwhile? Well, as Virgil tells us, meanwhile Time is flying, flying never to return. In brief, a one-way trip where we all share the same destination if not the same estimated time of departure.

And so, the first piece I ever published for money dealt, among other things, with the brevity of life. And, at age fifteen, much earlier, in the summer, in a house surrounded by hills and mountains overlooking the city of Saltillo, Coahuila, I also wrote about the brevity of life, and I included water, an irrigation stream that carried and spread the blood of two *campesinos* who attempted to escape a pursuing horseman intent on impressing them into military service.

In this last instance, I had a vague idea of what I was doing, but as vague as it was, it was an idea I meant to pursue. When the first published piece came out, some well-intentioned soul told me it revealed, and I quote, "the fatalism of the Mexican race." To paraphrase Oscar Wilde, "One needs a heart of stone not to laugh at such people."

Here's a small digression: Writing and publishing usually carry with them a certain amount of luck. My good luck came when the fatalism banner was neither hoisted nor waved for all to see. This is not to mean that students will not come up and ask me (invariably and almost uniformly) why it is that I mention death so often. I imagine they've counted the instances in the book they've read, and I can only imagine that their instructor pointed out this aspect to them. Worse, perhaps made them count the number of direct and indirect mentions in their notebooks.

My defense? None. The published books, as we all know, belong to the buyer, not to the writer.

End of digression.

Now, the Baroque also concerns itself with beauty, as do I. But unlike the Classics, the Baroque realized that beauty is impermanent, a part of life and thus transitory. What finally did it for me in this regard is a long poem by a Spanish nobleman said to be in love with the wife of the Emperor Charles V; it's a moving piece of writing and the disenchantment he writes of could only come from one who loved someone so much that to see the loved object ravaged by time and by death could produce the powerful lines that convinced the reader of the inescapable fate that awaits us all. Death, after all, is the supreme expression of the ephemeral. It is there, hidden, but present in everything that is fresh and beautiful . . . there's anxiety there, as we say in Spanish, *un amargo deleite*, a sweet sorrow; not unlike Juliet's parting words to Romeo, and the end that waited patiently for both of them.

And so, armed with some healthy skepticism, (another Baroque element for it recognizes that riches and ostentation are also transitory) I decided to write the novel I've been working on for over twenty years. I would construct an imaginary world where appearances would affirm themselves as reality. Where masks, a favorite usage of the Baroque, and cynicism, tempered by satire, would foster the illusion of permanence held by the inhabitants of this imagined world despite the fact that their illusions of power, wealth and control would be broken time and again.

The same characters would then appear, disappear and reappear; they would occupy different bodies and genders, different faces and ages, but always remaining in character. Thus, to define these characters would be difficult because of the eternal conflict familiar to us all: to be or to seem to be. And it would be a complicated game these characters would play and thus full of surprises. Who, then, would be wearing the mask?

Writing in this manner, I thought, would not be a flat picture with a disappearing point of perception. It was and is more like a stage, as in the novel *Rites and Witnesses,* which is clearly labeled "A Comedy." The first part consists of ritualized ceremonies and the second is populated by witnesses who affect or are affected by the rites and then, in the middle of the two parts, from beginning to end, a series of conversations that are the consequences of those rites and are related to some of the witnesses. Intercalated conversations that disrupt and are meant to disrupt, by their private reality, both the rites and the witnesses.

So instead of a flat picture, or a horizontal one, *Rites and Witnesses,* attempts to recover a vertical plane because several games are at play here aside from the pleasure of reading a challenging work. Its verticality, then, shows heaven and hell, but hell intercalated with earth and hence a conquest, of sorts, of space.

Writing in Spanish, at other times in English, at other times giving different versions of the same novel in one language or in the other, and always trying to produce a linguistic tension, the different values attained point toward some significance that I myself am trying to explain. The structures in this long novel are complex the familiar classic linearity, but substituted and invaded by complicated forms. Not as superfluous ornaments, but rather as part of the novelistic art itself—fundamental to artistic beauty, as I see it. And there must be artistic enhancement to all of this if it is to succeed, and in this regard I am quoting one of the great theorists of the Baroque, Baltazar Gracián.

There is also the tendency to unify a thousand and one strings, and trifles, too, but by this heaping of things, the constant reader/ participant associates events and characters into some organic whole—and the events, and such is life, are often contradictory. Additionally, I don't often go or try for an expression of direct significance but usually settle for different meanings which once again produce contradictions.

The readers of the work, and some have seen this already, gather that this vision of fusion is a reality; or, they may see this vision as a duality. In short, another paradox. That is, looking at that which is real is looking at something which is in conflict, and conflict lies at the basis of the Baroque; that is, the discovery of the interior conflict of mankind.

And so, the characters, the objects, the background and the actions are seldom described—they are suggested—and thus they blend with and are confused at times, and it's through the use of certain allusions which allow the characters and their actions not to be described but to be reflected through the eyes of other characters as if one looked at a mirror—but again not the mirror of the nineteenth-century Realists, but another mirror where reality is both refracted and reflected: imagine a still pool of water reflecting the blue sky, suddenly birds fly over the water, and you see the pool and you see the birds reflected in it; and, at the same time, you see the birds and interspersed, as they fly, you see the blue pond, but this time it's the sky, not the pond.

Multiple sensations, or, simply, the Baroque. Exaggerations, hyperbole, the occasional use of mixed syntax, antithesis, anaphoras, zeugmas for whatever effect, a surprise here and there, conciseness of presentation and degrees of difficulty to challenge the reader, all of these elements, if not unique to the Baroque, appear over and over as part of the writing of the novel which, incidentally, is called the *Klail City Death Trip Series.*

So, contradiction—two dualities which are then unified to present a vision, even if not a reality, of fusion, of vertical space—have found a repository in a person who has been a son and a father, a brother, a soldier, a civil servant, a high school teacher, an office manager, a sales manager, a laborer in a chemical plant with degree in hand and finally, a writer.

Not, then, a straightforward classic life but rather one full of curves, of vistas not always clarified nor clearly seen, and as always, an ongoing student and teacher who tries not to be taken in by the apparent permanence of things. And, finally, a piece of advice: when it comes to U.S. Hispanics, we're not all what we seem to be.

STORIES

ES EL AGUA
(1999)

Me llamo Fructuoso Alaniz García y así me bautizaron en las tierras de los Buenrostro por ser el día de mi santo, el día 21 de enero. En inglés, según mi nieta Lucía, mi nombre significa *bountiful*, es decir, productivo. Bien puede ser. De mi parte, me parece que eso encaja bien, ya que aquel que así se llama se le haya destinado a trabajar la tierra —y no sólo eso, no, sino también que el que labra le da vida a la tierra para que ella —la tierra— devuelva parte de la vida en cereales y en todo tipo de grano, en verduras, sí, y en fruta como recompensa para aquel que preparó la tierra y presenció la siembra brotar casi de la nada sino con la esperanza y con un manojo de semilla. Eso sí es que ser productivo.

Cuando trabajo en tierra ajena, la labro igual como si fuera mi propia parcela. No hay, ni veo diferencia alguna, no. La tierra es la tierra y al fin y al cabo —o cuando se nos acabe la música, como decimos por acá— uno deja el terreno para la siguiente persona. Pero hay que dejarla limpia, podada y lista para aquel que también viene como uno, lleno de esperanza y con ese manojo de semilla que le dije.

Yo soy de aquí, del Valle, fronterizo norteño igual que mi padre, igual que el abuelo, el bisabuelo y el tatarabuelo. Mexicano, sí, pero estadounidense de nacimiento, igual que ellos. Hace muchos años, allá cuando andaba en los 19 años de edad, en el año 1918, me mandaron a Francia; pero aquí me tiene usted. Volví y a trabajar, se ha dicho. Dos de mis primos, José Antonio y Francisco García no volvieron. Mi nieta Lucía —ah, y ella también trabajó la tierra hasta la edad de 17— ella dice que a los primos se les recuerda —¿será esa la palabra? ¿Se les recuerda? Bueno, Lucía dice que se les recuerda en Austin, la capital del estado. Sí, fíjese, en un estadio en la universidad donde los jóvenes juegan fútbol. Ella notó unas placas de metal en ese estadio, luego anotó los nombres y el dónde y cuándo murieron, y sí, son los mismos José Antonio y Francisco García —de eso no hay duda. Qué cosas, ¿verdad, usted? Yo no tenía idea que allá se les honrara. Pues, sí, yo también estuve en Francia —y esa tierra estaba cansada, me acuerdo bien— pero se repuso con el tiempo para proveer a la gente. ¡Je! Le diré algo que es muy de la tierra, profesor. Dios santísimo ya no esta haciendo más tierra. Es más, la tierra no se mueve ni se va. Allí está, lista para que la trabajen —y hay que trabajarla, ni para que andarse con rodeos.

Yo he trabajado la tierra en los estados de Minesota, Michigan, Ojayo, lugares lejos del Valle. En mis días atravesábamos el estado de Texas cruzando por el pueblo de Texarkana —de allí cruzábamos la línea divisoria para llegar al estado de Arkansó; lugar de malas carreteras en esos días. De ahí entrábamos a Poplar Bluf, en el estado de Misuri. Nos íbamos rumbo al sol sale, hasta cruzar el río Misisipí, para llegar a Cairo, en Ilinoy. Después le picábamos pa'l norte, hasta llegar a un pueblucho que esa gente llama Kankakí. Cierro los ojos y lo veo. De ahí le colábamos al este, rumbo a Reynolds, Indiana —eso queda en la ruta 420— y para acabar, subíamos al pleno norte, a New Búfalo, en Michigan. Viaje de tres/cuatro días con sus noches.

Bueno, una vez en Michigan, a cosechar la ciruela, la cereza, la uva, fruta suave y blanda. Pero, si le seguíamos al este de Michigan, recogíamos pepinos en Pinconing o el betabel o remolacha, y si nos íbamos al sur, caíamos en Ojayo donde se da mucho el tomate.

Bueno, esto ocurría así si uno hacía el viaje en su propio mueble, su carro propio, ¿no? Pero, si nos llevaban por contrato nos montaban en los camiones de los granjeros mismos y nos íbamos donde nos llevaran. Había veces que nos juntabamos en Júpeston, en Ilinoy, y nos separábamos allí. Unos amigos y parientes nuestros trabajaron por años por una sola familia de granjeros en el estado de Iowa; una familia, sí. Esa gente se dedicaba a cultivar flores y se necesitaba gente especial para desempeñar ese tipo de trabajo. Nosotros también trabajamos allá unas siete u ocho temporadas, ya no me acuerdo bien a bien. Los años se me corren, ¿sabe?

Mi mujer y yo, y ella también hacía los viajes, trabajamos juntos en los campos más de 27 años, y una vez buscamos trabajo en el estado de Wyomin que queda cerca del Canadá. Trabajamos con gente que viajaba desde Laredo, Texas. Mi mujer murió hace 10 años . . . nuestro único hijo, Marcos, falleció hace los cinco años contados en un accidente cuando el camión de transporte se estrelló contra un tren. Eso ocurrió en Monón, Indiana. Mi nieta Lucía salió ilesa y ahora estudia en la Universidad en Austin. Mi nuera, Estéfana, enviudó y vive con nosotros. Pasa que mi mujer y yo la críamos desde que era niña. Esa Estéfana es una de las mejores y de las más rápidas en la poda de la lechuga y su empaque. También se defiende en inglés, lo lee y lo escribe. Su prima, Isaura, es profesora normal y da sus clases durante los veranos en la escuelita que construimos de las ojas de palmeras. Ella misma compra los lápices y las tabletas de escribir, y así les enseña a leer, escribir y las cifras a los chicos. Lo hace porque ella misma dice que es necesario que se haga, de vez en cuando vienen varias de sus amigas y le ayudan, pero no importa, llueva o truene, Isaura está allí todos los días. No falla.

Mi nieto, Balde, cuenta con 23 años y es dueño de un camión usado y junto con un amigo suyo que también es del Valle y que se llama Raúl Santoscoy, son socios en el negocio. Balde es el campeón en eso de amontonar pacas de paja y de ceno en el camión. Cuando los jóvenes hacen la competencia, los que conocen a Balde apuestan su dinero con él. Raúl conduce el camión y los dos se las agencian para firmar contratos para el transporte de mercancías en el norte de Texas, en ciudades como Amarillo, Pleinbiew, lugares que nosotros del Valle llamamos *el norte*. Balde es el hermano mayor de mi nieta Lucía y él le manda dinero para sus estudios. "Mi hermana es un ejemplo", dice Balde y se enorgullece por los estudios que lleva su hermana, nosotros también estamos orgullecidos de Balde porque es un hombrecito hecho y derecho que no le tiene miedo al trabajo.

Tenemos un dicho aquí en el Valle: es el agua. El agua del Río Grande. Tú le perteneces al agua, pero el agua te pertenece a ti también. No importa dónde trabajemos, siempre volvemos a la frontera, al Valle. Es el agua.

El Valle tiene sus encantos, tierra dura, sí, pero esa es tierra de pan llevar, y uno tiene que ser más fuerte que la tierra y el trabajo. Y el Valle es diferente de otras partes de Texas y nosotros nos distinguimos porque somos de allí. Por eso, cuando vamos a otro Valle, el Yákima en el estado de Washington, o el Güilámet en Oregón, para la cosecha del lúpulo o a Nampa, en Aidajó, es como estar en casa. ¿Por qué? Porque los que viven allí eran originarios del Valle, sí. Y, y, y los chicos que en su vida han puesto pie en el Valle, dicen que son del Valle porque sus padres son de allí y así, los chicos saben de dónde son. Saber quién es uno es algo especial.

Esto está cambiando, pero todo cambia, es el son de la vida. Le daré un ejemplo: cuando mi mujer y yo y nuestros amigos trabajábamos en los algodones, y esto es solamente un ejemplo, pizcábamos algodón en el Valle de junio a agosto. Entonces, el dueño mandaba herir la tierra con el arado en septiembre por ley del estado. De ahí nos montábamos para ir a los algodones en el centro de Texas o al oeste del estado a lugares como Brawnfil o La

Mesa. A veces salíamos para Arkansó o Misuri para el algodón y le dábamos hasta Tenesí si se terciaba —pero ya no en estos últimos veinte años— ahora casi todo es cosa de maquinaria; pero con todo eso, las máquinas no pueden hacerlo todo, no. Todavía se necesita la mano de obra, el ojo humano que sabe y que puede distinguir. La maquinaria no se enorgullece por su trabajo, le es imposible. Pero uno sí se enorgullece por su trabajo. Eso de trabajar la tierra es asunto duro, en eso no hay sorpresa. Lo molestoso, y lo vergonzante, también, es dónde uno tiene que vivir en el mesoeste del país, en carpas o en gallineros; y esos son los peores. No siempre es así, pero con una vez basta para el recuerdo. Pero uno se aguanta, uno sobrevive, y hasta aguantamos y sobrevivimos el racismo, el prejuicio social de todos, y hasta por parte de los nuestros que nos menosprecian. Pero yo no puedo cambiar el mundo y Dios no quiere encargarse, como decimos.

Pero tampoco nos rajamos, no nos rendimos, no alzamos los brazos como los prisioneros. No. No nos rajamos y ya.

Pero, después de tanto trabajo y de viajes aquí y viajes allá, volvemos al Valle donde nos espera otra temporada de trabajo. Es el agua.

¡Je! Esos que aseguran que el trabajo es de beneficio pa'l cuerpo y saludable y todo eso, no saben de qué se trata la cosa. El trabajo rudo y duro está de la patada, y lo llaman duro porque eso es lo que es.

Te aplasta y hasta te mata. Pero también hay orgullo, orgullo de necios, quizás, pero una familia trabajadora se enorgullece porque trabaja y porque desempeña su trabajo como Dios manda. Al fin, como en todo, el trabajo se acaba.

Era como cuando estuve en Francia. Uno estaba allí hasta el día que alguien vino y dijo: "Vámonos ya. Vámonos a casa". Y así era como cuando uno se encontraba en Indiana, en Iowa, o en las bandas del río Rojo en Minesota. Uno estaba allí, en el jale como le llamamos al trabajo, y entonces alguien venía y decía: "Vámonos pa' la casa. Vámonos pa' Texas. Pa'l Valle".

Sí, es el agua.

ES EL AGUA
(2000)

M y name is Fructuoso Alaniz García, and I was so named for my Saint's Day, the twenty-first day of January; in English, according to my granddaughter Lucía, my name means *bountiful, productive*. Myself, I find it proper that one so named should be chosen to work the land, to know it and to give it life so that it—the land—return part of that life in grain and cereal, in vegetables and, yes, in fruits of labor and of bounty to that person who prepared the land and watched the crops grow from nothing but a hope and a handful of seeds.

When I work my land, the one I own, I work it the same way I work somebody else's land. It makes no difference; none, really. Land is land, and when all is said and done, or, as we say, when the music is over, one leaves the terrain, *el terreno*, for somebody else to occupy. But, one must leave the land clean, weeded and ready for that somebody else who comes to it with that hope and that handful of seeds I spoke of.

I'm from here, the Valley; a northbank borderer like my father, like his father, and his, too. A Mexican, of course, but an American by birth, yes. And once, when I was nineteen years old, in 1918, I was sent to France, but as you can see, I came back. Two of my cousins, José Antonio and Francisco García, did not. My granddaughter Lucía—and she, too, worked the land until she was seventeen years old—my granddaughter says that my cousins are remembered—is that the word?—*remembered?*—anyway, my granddaughter says that they are remembered in Austin, the capital. Yes, they are in a park at the University where the young men play football. She saw the metal plaques in that park, took down the dates of where and when they died, and yes, they are the same José Antonio and Francisco García, all right. That's something I didn't know about, the memorial plates. Yes, I was in France, and one thing about land, Professor, God's not making anymore, it isn't going anywhere, and you got to work it, that's all there is to it.

I've worked the land in Minnesota, Michigan, Ohio, places like that. We used to drive up from the Valley to Texarkana, Texas across to Arkansas, they had some bad roads there in my day, and on to Poplar Bluff in Missouri. From there we'd go east to the Mississippi River to Cairo, Illinois, and then north to Kankakee; from there, east again to Reynolds, Indiana, that's on Route 420, and then north to New Buffalo, Michigan. Well, once in Michigan, we'd pick plums, cherries, grapes; soft fruit. But, if we'd drove on to east Michigan, we'd pick cucumbers in Pinconning or beets and then if we'd go south, to Ohio, we'd pick tomatoes there.

This could be done if we drove, if we had a car of our own. If we went by truck, on a contract, then we'd go where they'd take us. Sometimes we'd meet in Hoopeston, Illinois, and separate from there. Some friends and relatives of ours from the Valley worked for years for one family in Iowa; one family. They owned a nursery, and they needed special people for that; I worked there, too, seven or eight seasons, I guess.

My wife, she made the trips, too; we travelled together for twenty-seven years, and once we worked in Wyoming with some people who came up from Laredo, Texas. My wife died ten years ago . . . our son, Marcos, died two years ago, in a truck-train accident in Monon, Indiana. My granddaughter Lucía was unhurt, and she's a student in Austin, at the university. My son's widow, Estéfana, lives in our house, and she runs it now; my wife and I raised her from childhood, and she's been part of the family since she was a baby. Estéfana is one of the best and one of the fastest lettuce cutters and packers in the Valley—she's as good as some men I know and better than some others. And, she can read and write English, too. Her cousin, Isaura, is a schoolteacher, and in the summertime, Isaura teaches school for free in the school we built out in the field. She buys pencils and writing tablets, and she teaches reading and writing and the numbers to the kids. She does it because she says it is necessary; once in a while some friends come and help her, but no matter what, Isaura is there every day. Working . . .

My grandson, Balde, is twenty-three-years old, and he already owns a used truck; he and a friend of his, a Valley boy named Raúl Santoscoy, is his partner. Balde is a champion hay stacker, yes, he is; in competition, too. Raúl drives the truck and the two of them contract for hay hauling in North Texas: Amarillo, Plainview; what we call "up north," *el norte*. Balde is my granddaughter's older brother, and he sends her money to Austin for her schooling. She's an example, he says, and he's proud of his sister; well, so are we, but Balde is also a fine young man who is not afraid of hard work.

We have a saying here in the Rio Grande Valley: *es el agua*; it's the water, the Río Grande water. It claims you, you understand? It's yours and you belong to it, too. No matter where we work, we always come back. To the border, to the Valley.

Es el agua, yes.

The Valley is a good place. It's hard, sure—*seguro*—but there's farm work, and one just has to be harder than the work. And the Valley is different, too, and it makes us different, somehow. When we leave it to go to the Yakima Valley or to Oregon for the hops or to Nampa in Idaho, we're home there, too. Why? Well, because the workers there are Valley people, yes. And, and, and the kids who have never been to the Valley say they're from there because that's where their folks are from. *Es el agua*; their parents talk about the Valley, see, and the kids know.

This is changing, of course, but everything changes, it is in the nature of things. I'll show you. When my wife and our friends picked cotton, and this is just an example, we picked in the Valley from June to August, and then the owner plowed the ground in September. Well, by late August some of us'd go to Central Texas to pick or to West Texas in October and November, to places like Brownfield and Lamesa. Sometimes we'd go to Arkansas or to Missouri for cotton and to Tennessee, but not anymore and not for some twenty years now; machines do it, but they can't do everything. No, you still need *la mano de obra*, the human hand, the eye to see and to distinguish. Machines don't take pride in what they do, they can't. . . . But we did, and do. Yes.

Work is work, and most of it is hard; but that's expected. What's a bother, and shameful, too, is where one has to live in the American Midwest: in our cars or trucks, or on the ground, in a *carpa*— a tent—or in chicken and turkey coops; these are the worst. Yes. Terrible . . . it isn't always like that, no, but even once is enough, believe me. But one endures, one survives, and one even survives and endures *racismo* and *prejuicio*—racism, prejudice—from everybody, even our own. But I can't change it and God won't, as we say . . . *Pero tampoco nos rajamos*—we won't crack, we won't throw up our hands and say: "I give up." No. *No nos rajamos y ya*; we won't give up, and that's it. . . . But, after all the work and travel, it's back to the Valley for more work. *Es el agua*, yes.

Ha! Those who claim hard work never killed anybody are fooling themselves and their friends. Hard work is hard, that's why they call it that; it's killing, but there's a certain kind of pride, foolish pride, perhaps, and understandable, too, but a family is proud of what it does and of what it can *do*. It's like when I was in France sixty years ago, one was *there*, and *stayed* there until they said,

"Let's go. Let's go home." And that is the way it is when we are in Indiana or Iowa or in the Red River Valley of Minnesota, one is there, then someone says, "Let's go home. To Texas. Home. To the Valley."

Es el agua.

EL PUÑAL DE BORGES

(2005)

E n esa fina traducción que Norman Thomas de Giovanni publicó (con la colaboración del mismo Borges) hace años en la
revista semanal *The New Yorker* se habla sobre un puñal en el
escritorio de JLB, regalo que le vino por manos de su amigo
Evaristo Carriego. Borges ofrece queja y lamento por el desuso
violento de dicho puñal. En vez de abrir cuerpos violentamente (se
menciona un tigre en el poema) su papel es el de abrir cartas y
sobres; uso ignoble, en la estimación de Borges.

Hay cierto parecido a lo de Hemingway quien nos cuenta del
leopardo congelado en las alturas del monte Kilimanjaro. El
escritor norteamericano pregunta que qué era lo que buscaba o que
pretendía el leopardo en la cima del monte más alto de África y la
pregunta cabe ¿cómo llegó el puñal de Borges en manos del ahora
finado Rigo Contreras, nativo y originario del condado de Belken
en el valle bajo del Río Grande de Texas? ¿Qué hacía el puñal en
esos lares? ¿Cómo llegó a tal paradero?

Ahora que soy su dueño me parece que la historia debe contarse:

La última vez que fui a casa de Contreras, le pregunté cómo y cuándo le había caído el puñal en sus manos.

"Nada de misterio, ¿sabes? Le escribí al poeta, expresé curiosidad en el puñal, alabé el poema en el cual Borges dijo que había colaborado con de Giovanni, y de repente, mientras le escribía, y además, ¿qué iba a perder, verdad?, se lo pedí. Así, sin más ni menos.

"No ofrecí pagar los gastos de correo ya que eso se me hacía algo vulgar. Casi un insulto ya que se pasaba de importunarlo, ¿no? La carta en el buzón, y a esperar.

"Me contesta, y tú te puedes imaginar la sorpresa. Lo fuerte del plato era que me ofrecía el puñal. Y aquí lo cito: '¿Sigue?' rezaba la carta, '¿sigue usted interesado en el puñal? ¿Lo utilizaría a otros usos y no sólo para abrir cartas o cosas por el estilo?'"

Contreras, y lo veo como si fuera ayer, tomó un sorbo largo de su cerveza, me vio, casi descaradamente, e hizo un leve meneo de cabeza.

"Qué atrevimiento, ¿verdad? Sí, sí, te lo veo en la cara. Sí, sentado en ese sofá y pensando que cuándo vendrá la gente uniformada para conducirme nuevamente al manicomio en San Antonio o donde sea que esté ese lugar donde guardan a los locos peligrosos. Te leo como un libro para chicos del kínder".

Pasan unos momentos y le pregunto: "¿Y las celdas? ¿Bien?"

"Ni me acuerdo ya, fíjate".

Le dejé saber que después de esos diez años, que acababa de releer el *Klail City News Enterprise* nuevamente. Que había seguido la historia del puñalamiento del joven Calixto Cepeda. Que, ahora, aunque venía a su casa como viejo amigo y no como jefe inspector de policía. . . .

"Bueno, sí, pero como amigo empapado de curiosidad, ¿no es así?"

Me encogí de brazos. "¿Por qué lo apuñalaste? Ni lo conocías, que digamos. Por lo que investigué en aquel tiempo, no había pleito con la familia Cepeda. Y fue la violencia, Rigo, eso fue lo que daba pavor. Y sin provocación alguna".

Sin querer, me estremecí y Contreras lo tomó como desaprobacion, por decirlo así.

"Tuve que hacerlo, ¿sabes?"

Los filósofos nos dicen que una respuesta sencilla y críptica ofrece claridad y obscuridad, ya que a la vez ilumina y oculta.

"La cosa es que le escribiste a Borges, te manda el puñal, pasan los años, y luego, al aniversario de su muerte, te entras en el Aquí Me Quedo y sin palabra alguna, coges a Cepeda por detrás, le estiras por los cabellos, y exponiendo . . ."

"El cuello. Dílo. El cuello con todas sus venas y lo degollé. Cosa más fácil".

Le ofrecí un cigarrillo.

Tosió levemente. "Fue el puñal, Rafa. ¿Qué no lo ves? Mira, lo mantenía en una situación parecidísima a la de Borges, en el escritorio, sin hacer nada. Lo sacaba, sí, lo examinaba, le daba su brillo donde salía ese azul que despide el buen acero. Pero eso era todo. Allí estaba. Gastando su vida, en cuclillas y listo. Pero sin vida alguna. Nada. ¿Pero verdaderamente me entiendes lo que te digo?

"Ahora bien, no sería yo quien lo iba a diminuir y usarlo para abrir la cuenta del agua y la luz. Creo que me entiendes, ¿no? Era un tigre, sí, exactamente un tigre, animal acostumbrado a la violencia ¿y qué? ¡Ja! Da vergüenza. Lo tenía, allí, en ese escritorio. Soterrado. Diez años y más, de inactividad frustrante. ¿Para qué había molestado a Borges si no lo iba a usar, como se lo prometí? ¿De qué sirve un puñal?"

Antes de poder contestarle, Rigo Contreras alzó la mano.

"Me llamó, el puñal, ¿sabes? Habló conmigo".

"Me acuerdo bien, sí. Tu abogado convence al jurado que eras un enfermo y ahora, tres años más tarde, aquí en casa, como si nada".

"Me habló el puñal. Pero ¿tú qué vas a entender? Aún me llama, ¿sabes? Mira, no sé dónde ustedes del condado tienen ese puñal, pero de que es mío, que a mí me pertenece, que no te quepa duda alguna. Mi propiedad, un regalo, un regalo de uno de los mejores poetas de este siglo, y yo quiero que se me devuelva mi propiedad".

"Ajá. ¿Y si te habla de nuevo?"

"En verdad, no sabría qué decirte, Rafa".

"No, eso no vale. Me voy".

Con esto me dirigí a la puerta. "Adiós, Rigo".

La tosecita de nuevo. "No pasa mucha gente por aquí y de repente, tú. Esto sí que fue una sorpresa. ¿Y qué esperabas de mí? ¿Qué querías que te dijera? ¿A todo esto, qué te trajo aquí, eh? No podría haber sido esa amistad que dices. ¿A ver? ¿Qué?¿Qué?"

"Esto". Extendí la mano. Mi vieja escuadra del ejército, una Colt 45.

"Ah, bueno, ya que no me vas a dar el puñal, la pistola también puede servirme para algo".

"Esto es adiós, Rigo".

"¿Cómo que adiós?"

"El último, sí".

NICE CLIMATE, MIAMI
(2009)

The next day, a cloudless Monday after three days of thunderstorms, a bluer-than-blue sky and a white sun shimmered on a hamburger joint not far from Grant's tomb, when O'Hara hailed a cab: "Take the tunnel. We're going to La Guardia."

He bought a one-way fare to San Francisco for the following week. From there, he took a different cab, this one to Kennedy, where he bought two more one-way e-tickets: one to Montreal, the other to Miami.

Two days later, he went to Barney's at midmorning and paid cash for two lightweight summer suits, a pair of Chucks, a pair of Ray-Bans and some Oxford cloth shirts. He then bought a cashmere pullover.

"Here," he said to the clerk. "This is for my sister, Kathi Luckman. Here's her address. Here's a hundred, keep what's left."

"Thank you, sir."

On Thursday, a carry-on in hand, he took another cab, this one to Grand Central Terminus. Once there, he looked around for a moment, then headed for a rental unit nearest the east entrance.

Back in his Village apartment, he oiled and cleaned his Totter caliber 2.72—a keepsake once used by a woman, a Russian Mafia hitter out of Brighton Beach. Earlier that morning, O'Hara had spent three hours shredding his identity as John Rienzi, beginning with his driver's license, the credit and debit cards and on to his Social Security card. He then used his disposable cell to call the movers and remind them of the following morning's appointment. The next day, they pulled up to his apartment on time.

"That's it? The desk, the chair and six boxes?"

O'Hara nodded and gave the movers an address in Astoria. The apartment was not much different and just as bare.

"Here's a key to the new place. When you're through, leave it with the man at the corner bodega. Tell 'em it's from Rienzi. Got that?"

The driver nodded, took the money and looked at the tall man, who then handed him a fifty-dollar tip.

"Live it up. It's Friday."

At eight-thirty that evening, the humidity hovered in the thirties, with the temperature a couple notches past seventy degrees. O'Hara left the Astoria apartment and, taking an unhurried look at his few belongings, he locked the door and took the subway coming in from Twenty-Third Street/Ely Avenue. Crossing the river into Manhattan, he took the subway to Eighty-Sixth Street in Yorktown —the old German section. He then took a cab south to Midtown and stopped by a flower shop on Lexington.

Sure he wasn't being followed, a quick swipe to his upper lip removed the fake mustache. He then put on a pair of horn-rims.

Flowers, he thought, that's the ticket. A dozen gladiolas and another cab, this one to Sutton Place. He glanced at the bridge as three young, smartly dressed girls laughed when they saw the flowers. O'Hara smiled sheepishly. "You're right, they're for my wife. I've been a bad boy."

One of them pointed a slender index finger as if to say, "That's what you get. You ought to know better, a man your age." And she laughed gaily as O'Hara smiled and shrugged, as any middle-aged husband resigned to take whatever awaited him at home might do. They waved at him, and the three said, "Good luuuuck."

He smiled again and looked at his watch—five till nine. He hurried toward the river, and within seven minutes he stood on the corner of Fifty-Ninth Street. He'd written the apartment's address on the palm of his left hand: 362 E. 59th, Apt. 2-B.

He looked up. The light was faint in the apartment. He went back mentally to the layout of the place, and he crossed the street to wait. The woman appeared, fifty if a day, he thought, in a tailor-made coat. Ha! As usual, pulling on that overweight hairless dachshund. He made as if fumbling for his keys and, looking up, the woman smiled and opened the door for him.

"Thank you."

"Oh, it's no bother. Billy and I are going out for our walk. Come on, Bill."

O'Hara looked at the flowers: the best passport. He immediately pressed the elevator button to the second floor. Refurbished, the apartment building no longer had a firebox in the basement. O'Hara left the flowers in the elevator. He pocketed the horn-rims, turned right and stood in front of 2-B. He pressed his ear against the door. Not a sound. He frowned and checked his watch again: nine-fifteen; the woman had taken the dog for a walk; he's supposed to be in there.

O'Hara reached into his left-hand pocket, drew out a credit card and jiggled it. The door opened noiselessly. With his back to the wall, he crossed his arms and waited for his eyes to become accustomed to the faint darkness. The sofa, by the piano; to the left, the window with an impressive view of Midtown. The TV was at the furthest reach of the bedroom, and the john was . . . he heard a slight noise coming from the direction of the toilet. A faucet was turned off. Then he heard some steps, a sneeze followed by a cough and a clearing of the throat.

"It's him," he said to himself.

The man coughed again and blew his nose as he entered the room.

"Mr. Rusconi."

The man looked up. "Who are you? How'd you get in? And what do you want?"

"I'm a bit slow, Mr. Rusconi. I came to see you about a debt."

Rusconi blew into the wet handkerchief again, hesitated a bit and said, "Yeah. I suppose it's about the vig, right?"

O'Hara looked at him and shrugged.

"Hold it, hold it. Look, I can pay, yeah, really. Right now."

"A bit late. I've got my orders." With this, he showed him the Totter 2.72.

"Hey, what are you doing? If you kill me, I can't pay up, right?"

O'Hara shook his head slowly. "They don't want the money. The debt's been placed on the debit side. They'll eat it. It's a lesson to the others, that's all. A lesson."

"But, ah, we, ah, we, we can make an arrangement, you and me, right? I mean, well, really, you see . . . Can I sit down?"

"Sure. It's better that way. An arrangement? Sounds like a bribe. No, I can, but I won't. Besides, it's not to my advantage, if I can put it that way. I either kill you, or they'll come after me. Is that simple enough?"

"Oh, you're not a member of the Family, is that it? And you don't look Italian. A contract?" Rusconi rubbed his face. Money, he thought. That's the only thing these people understand. They've all got a price.

O'Hara smiled, as if he'd read Rusconi's mind. "What? You're going to offer me five thousand, is that it? Look, I'm getting twenty-five hundred, a freebie. You understand?"

"Sure, of course."

O'Hara interrupted him and laughed. "No, you don't. The silencer's a great friend, by the way. You won't hear a thing. C'mon, close your eyes."

Rusconi raised his hands and shook his head. "No. Twenty-five, what do you say? Twenty-five." Breathing hard now, Rusconi sneezed again. "Listen, no, no, listen to me. Fifty, how's that? Fifty thousand for you. Alone. Think on it. Fifty thousand. Right now." O'Hara turned and said, "To the bedroom. Move it. Now, take your pajamas off."

"What was that?"

"Take 'em off and throw 'em on the floor. Do it."

He aimed the Totter at Rusconi. "Unmake the bed, throw everything on the floor." His voice became colder: "To the john."

O'Hara pushed him and said, "In the shower. Turn it on."

Rusconi began to whimper.

A minute or so later, O'Hara said, "Okay, that's enough. Turn the water off. Forget the towel. The bedroom, let's go. No, don't dry off. Move it."

The phone.

"Let it ring. You've got an answering machine."

Rusconi hesitated as O'Hara raised the handgun.

A woman's voice. An apology for not having called sooner. "At Chapin's, tomorrow morning. Ten o'clock, don't forget. I'll wait, but don't make me wait too long, John."

After the click, Rusconi looked at O'Hara. "My wife."

"You're a bachelor, Rusconi. That machine mark the hour?"

Rusconi nodded and kept wringing his hands.

"Okay. The money. Where is it?"

Rusconi sneezed and signaled to an end table by the bed.

"That?"

"It doesn't look like it, but it's a safe. I had it made like that."

Rusconi looked at O'Hara as if trying to read his mind. "You really gonna let me go?"

"If it's fifty. Otherwise . . . "

"Hey, it's all I got on hand right now, but it's fifty, all right. Maybe even a little bit more."

"Stand by the wall there. Face it. Get your hands up."

Rusconi sneezed again. "I'm soaked. What'd you make me take a shower for?"

"Look at it this way: I walked in, you were in the shower, I held you up and I wounded you."

"What?"

"Look, this is a Totter 2.72, nine-millimeter with a special charge. If I hit the meat part, shoulder, leg, it doesn't matter, the bullet goes right through you. Got that? There'll be blood, but it won't be a serious wound. Now, turn around."

"No, I can't stand pain. No."

"Listen to me, Rusconi. I take the money and leave you to call a doctor, or I'll take the money and do the deed. Nothing to it."

"Not many big bills there, how're you gonna carry 'em?"

"Get one of your bags and stuff it in there. Hurry. Now, here's the story. The cops will come when you call them . . . you got anything else? This has to look like a robbery."

Rusconi crammed the money in and stopped. "My friend's earrings, a pearl necklace—nice—and some rings. Oh, and two pair of cufflinks she bought me. Cartier's, I think. They're in here."

"Good enough. Go on, fill it. You tell the cops that they . . . that they took a good amount of cash. You got that?"

Rusconi relaxed a bit and nodded. "There, I'll zip it."

"Good job."

"What do we do now?"

"Don't move, and listen carefully. Stand by the bed, leave the safe wide open. Good. Now, what will it be, an arm or a leg?"

"The arm, the left one. Be careful, please."

With a bored look on his face, O'Hara said, "Closer to the bed, I said. Stick your arm out. Good. You're not going to die, Rusconi. Look at me."

"Careful, okay?"

O'Hara took a deep breath, aimed and shot him in the heart. Rusconi fell on the bed, then slid off the silk sheets and onto the floor. O'Hara waited a few seconds, then used Rusconi's phone.

He looked at Rusconi again and said, "It's Rienzi."

"Just a moment, sir, I'll get my dad."

As he waited, he hefted the bag.

"Everything all right?"

"Yes, sir. And with a bonus. He offered me money. Something like eleven or twelve thousand. I've not counted it yet."

"Ha! Little chiseling Italian Jew. Look, take another two for you. You want someone to come by and pick you up?"

"No, sir, I think I'll take the route you gave me. Go down to Midtown, come back up again and down to Mulberry. How's that?"

"Forty-five minutes, you think?"

"Or less, yes, sir."

He walked casually to the phone plug and kicked it. Another casual look around as he headed for the door. Once outside, he stood in the shadows. Clear sailing, he said to himself. A man with a suitcase.

He walked the three blocks south and went downstairs, making his way to the subway platform. He waited there five minutes, walked up to Fifty-Seventh and stopped when he got to Madison.

He turned the corner, bag in hand and hailed a cab. "Grand Central. Go by Riverside."

"Riverside? That's kind of a long way."

"There's no hurry."

Fifteen minutes later and a few blocks from the station, he asked the cabbie to parallel park.

"You pronounce your name Achmed, do you?"

The exact pronunciation of his name made the cabbie smile. "It sure is, but the fares usually call me Atchmed."

"Well, Achmed, I'll walk from here. It's a nice, cool night. By the way, do you know if the trains run this late to Westchester County?"

"Oh, yeah. I think they go all the time."

A glance at the watch: ten on the dot. "A couple of twenties, Achmed."

"I'll help you with the bag." As the driver walked to the trunk, O'Hara drew the Trotter. He kept his eyes on the Arab and set it at the ready.

"Look, I found this on the seat. Is it yours?"

"Oh, no. We can't carry."

"I'll keep it, then."

He strolled by the newsstand and picked up a copy of that morning's Times. From there to the locker to pick up his clothes. A glance at his watch: ten-fifteen. He waited until ten-thirty, then stepped outside to hail a cab.

"JFK."

"Catching the red-eye, are you?"

"Business. Delta departure. Look, there's an extra fifty if you can make it in twenty minutes."

"From here, at this hour? Piece of cake."

O'Hara casually shoved the Totter under the seat and leaned back. He nodded and said to himself, "Nice climate, Miami."

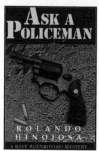

Ask a Policeman: A Rafe Buenrostro Mystery
Rolando Hinojosa
1998, 208 pages, Trade Paperback, ISBN: 978-1-55885-226-6,
$12.95

To solve a mystery of drug smuggling and murder on the Texas-Mexico border, Buenrostro leads a corps of bicultural sleuths in piercing the intrigue of a crime family apparently at war with itself.

"A page-turner, a quick and easy read." —*Dallas Morning News*

"Hinojosa skillfully lays out the different obstacles Buenrostro and his Mexican counterparts must overcome and he paints a textured portrait of the peculiar cultural amalgum formed at the border." —*Publishers Weekly*

Becky and Her Friends
Rolando Hinojosa
1989, 160 pages, Trade Paperback, ISBN: 978-1-55885-006-4,
$9.50

Becky Escobar takes the limelight in this novel in Hinojosa's Klail City Death Trip series.

"The Klail City Death Trip series continues to evolve both as a criticism and a celebration; altogether the novels constitute a lovingly accurate recreation of Valley people, politics, speech, social attitudes—even the weather."
—*Austin American-Statesman*

Dear Rafe / Mi querido Rafa
Rolando Hinojosa
Introduction by Manuel Martín-Rodríguez
2005, 256 pages, Trade Paperback
ISBN: 978-1-55885-456-7, $14.95

In the weeks leading up to the Democratic primary in Belken County, Jehu Malacara chronicles the political rabble-rousing of Klail City's wealthiest citizens in letters to his cousin, Rafe Buenrostro. Part epistolary, part mystery, this volume combines for the first time the English- and Spanish-language versions of the novel that creates a fictitious community that *The New York Times* compared to Faulkner's Yoknapatawpha and Márquez's Macondo.

"Although his sharp eye and accurate ear capture a place, its people and a time in a masterly way, his work goes far beyond regionalism. He is a writer for all readers, and *Dear Rafe* . . . is a delight in any league." —*The New York Times Book Review*